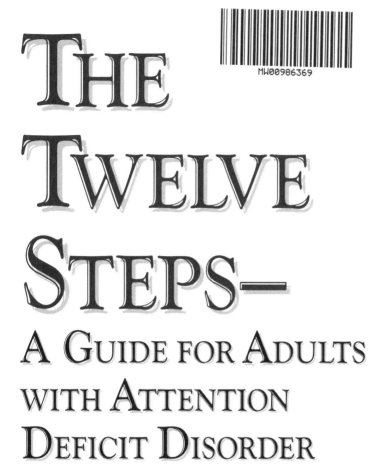

THE TWELVE STEPS—
A GUIDE FOR ADULTS WITH ATTENTION DEFICIT DISORDER

Friends in Recovery

RPI Publishing, Inc.
San Diego

Published by
RPI Publishing, Inc.
P.O. Box 44
Curtis, WA 98538
(360)-245-3386

The Twelve Steps are reprinted with permission of Alcoholics Anonymous World Services, Inc. Permission to reprint and adapt the Twelve Steps does not mean that AA has reviewed or approved the contents of this publication, nor that AA agrees with the views expressed herein. AA is a program of recovery from alcoholism only—use of the Twelve Steps in connection with programs and activities which are patterned after AA, but which address other problems, does not imply otherwise.

For the purpose of this book, the word "alcohol" in Step One has been changed to read "ADD," the word "Him" in Steps Three, Seven and Eleven have been changed to "God", and "alcoholics" in Step Twelve has been changed to read "others."

NOTICE: This book is designed to provide information regarding the subject matter covered. It is provided with the understanding that the publisher and author are not engaged in rendering individualized professional services. The processes and questions are intended for group or individual study, and not designed to be a substitute for professional therapy when such help is necessary.

ISBN 0-941405-35-4   pbk

Printed in the United States of America

10 9 8 7 6 5 4 3 2

THE TWELVE STEPS OF ALCOHOLICS ANONYMOUS

1. We admitted we were powerless over alcohol—that our lives had become unmanageable.
2. Came to believe that a power greater than ourselves could restore us to sanity.
3. Made a decision to turn our will and our lives over to the care of God *as we understood Him.*
4. Made a searching and fearless moral inventory of ourselves.
5. Admitted to God, to ourselves, and to another human being the exact nature of our wrongs.
6. Were entirely ready to have God remove all these defects of character.
7. Humbly asked Him to remove our shortcomings.
8. Made a list of all persons we had harmed, and became willing to make amends to them all.
9. Made direct amends to such people wherever possible, except when to do so would injure them or others.
10. Continued to take personal inventory and when we were wrong promptly admitted it.
11. Sought through prayer and meditation to improve our conscious contact with God, *as we understood Him,* praying only for knowledge of His will for us and the power to carry that out.
12. Having had a spiritual awakening as the result of these steps, we tried to carry this message to alcoholics, and to practice these principles in all our affairs.

Other Books by Friends in Recovery

The 12 Steps for Adult Children

The 12 Steps—A Way Out

The Twelve Steps for Christians

The Twelve Steps—A Spiritual Journey

The Twelve Steps—A Key for Living
with Attention Deficit Disorder

This book is dedicated to our family members and friends who have suffered from addiction and have been diagnosed with ADD. We sincerely hope that they find the same peace and serenity through the Twelve Steps that we found.

TABLE OF CONTENTS

FOREWORD

As women with ADD, we struggled for years with symptoms of undiagnosed attention deficit disorder. When we were diagnosed with ADD, each of us experienced a profound sense of relief. Finally we had a framework within which we could make sense of the difficulties we had encountered throughout our lives. We had a basis for understanding why it had been so difficult for us to measure up to the expectations of parents, teachers, spouses, friends, and all the other significant people in our lives. And we had the information we needed to start making changes in our lives. We believed everything would be okay now.

Energized by the relief of knowing about our ADD, we immersed ourselves in "getting better" and gaining control over this uninvited companion in our lives, once and for all. We worked hard to educate ourselves about ADD and became "walking encyclopedias" on the subject. We explored treatment options and began connecting with fellow ADDers throughout the country. We attacked our organizational systems, diligently making to-do lists and establishing personal goals. We did make progress; our lives became more manageable, and we began feeling more optimistic about the future. Gradually, however, as many newly diagnosed ADD adults discover sooner or later, feelings of anger, sadness, regret, and depression began surfacing. We said to ourselves, "Why us? Why does life have to be so difficult? Why do we have to work so hard at managing our lives? Why can't we be 'normal'?"

What we both came to realize was that an important piece was missing from our puzzle. We were trying to obtain balance in our lives, but we hadn't faced our feelings and resentments about having to live with a condition over which we had no control—one that would affect our lives forever. We found this realization extremely painful, but it was essential for our subsequent and ongoing recovery.

The book you are about to read explores the process of grief each of us had to ultimately experience in our respective journeys toward greater self-awareness and self-acceptance. Although *The Twelve Steps—A Guide for Adults with ADD* is based on the Twelve Steps of Alcoholics Anonymous, don't be misled. You don't have to be an addict to gain value from the principles of the Twelve Steps. The spiritual guidance offered by the Twelve Steps is a positive addition to education, medication, and therapy, and can be invaluable to adults with ADD. The Steps offer a way to find balance, peace, and serenity—qualities that are usually absent in the lives of adults with ADD.

We know from our personal experience that ADD is about dysregulation in many areas of our lives; it's about extremes of behavior and emotions; it's about varied dysfunctional coping strategies that people develop during decades of living with the chaos and out-of-control feelings that ADD creates. It's about all kinds of self-destructive addictive behaviors, many of which can be managed only within the framework of knowledge about ADD.

Our task as adults with ADD is to minimize the impact of being out of balance—the experience of living in a state of internal and external chaos. We need to find ways to bring order to our lives, whether or not they include substance abuse. Although we may not be addicted to a substance, we often have many of the behaviors that are common in addicts. For this reason, the Twelve Steps offer hope and encouragement to adults with ADD in the same way that they do for addicts. They offer a spiritual discipline for finding balance when our lives are out of control.

We believe this new book provides a unique perspective and approach to living with ADD. It's not about *doing*—tips, to-do lists, techniques, strategies, etc. It's about *being*—about simplifying one's life and becoming balanced and centered. It's a way to become self-aware and self-accepting—a way to find peace with oneself, others, and the universe.

We believe this book can answer many of the questions that continue to plague you and make your life unmanageable. If your life is touched by attention deficit disorder and you seek more balance, you owe it to yourself to read this book.

KATE KELLY AND PEGGY RAMUNDO
Coauthors of *You Mean I'm Not Lazy, Stupid or Crazy?*

Peggy Ramundo is a teacher now working as a consultant with ADD children and adults. She conducts workshops and lectures on ADD around the country. Kate Kelly is a clinical specialist in psychiatric nursing who currently gives presentations and leads therapy groups for ADD adults. Together, they were early pioneers of the Attention Deficit Disorder Council of Greater Cincinnati. Ms. Ramundo also cofounded the NIADD, the National Institute for Attention Deficit Disorder, in 1990.

ABOUT THIS BOOK

The Twelve Steps—A Guide for Adults with Attention Deficit Disorder was written as an important spiritual resource for adults with ADD. Although education, counseling, structure, coaching, and medication are effective treatment methods, they do not address the spiritual needs of adults with ADD.

The Twelve Steps, originally developed for alcoholics, provide the spiritual foundation and structure for this book. Although many people believe that the Twelve Steps are only for addicts, they are first and foremost a spiritual guide and discipline for anyone who is struggling with life's difficulties. The healing power of the Twelve Steps comes from maintaining contact with a loving Higher Power, who can do for us what we cannot do for ourselves. This spiritual program is a key that has opened the door to freedom for countless millions of people across the world.

The main emphasis of the book is to help people learn to use the Steps as a guide for developing a healthier lifestyle by applying spiritual principles. Each Step includes a Step review and an exercise to help readers identify their specific issues and begin the process of sharing openly with others. Although the text provides information and education, it does not impart technical or medical information about ADD. Instead, it focuses on spiritual tools for living with the symptoms and behaviors that are present in adults with ADD.

Included in the appendices are guidelines for facilitators, self-help resources, formats for meetings, and read-aloud materials for the meetings. Also included are suggestions for choosing a sponsor, recovery partner, or coach.

A number of supportive and loving friends appear in each Step and offer information relevant to the material being covered. These friends are a team of supporters who will be there to encourage, educate, and cheer you along the way. Allow them to introduce themselves.

I'm going to appear with a prayer at the end of each Step to help you keep your spiritual focus. Real help and hope comes from your Higher Power—the loving source of your strength, sanity, and self-esteem. God's grace, love, and power can and will change your life.

I'm here to help you keep a positive and winning attitude. I know many of the plays that can keep you in the game and on your feet. I plan to give you lots of encouragement and friendly support. I've been where you are, and I want to share some of the strategies that work for me.

I'm one of those old-timers whom I'm sure you've heard about. I've been in a twelve-step program for years, and am full of practical wisdom and counsel for you. I'll be sharing my experience, strength, and hope with you and encouraging you to stay on the path to peace and seren

I'm here to help you build structure, routine, and ritual into your life. ADD tends to leave you distracted, scattered, and confused at times, and I know how helpful structure and routine can be. My hope is to help you discover and develop the type of structure that will keep you focused, more productive, and happier.

I'm here to offer facts about ADD that will teach you what the disorder is and how it can affect your life. You will do much better if you know as much as possible about ADD and the effect it has on you and those around you.

I'm going to give you some sound medical advice about taking care of yourself so you can deal more effectively with your ADD. In addition to talking about medication, I will provide some helpful hints for keeping yourself in good physical condition. I'll be stressing the importance of diet and exercise as part of your treatment.

When you see me, it's time to pat yourself on the back. I'll be talking as if I were you and saying things that will help boost your self-esteem. I hope to help you erase the negative tapes in your head that reinforce the wrong messages you hear about yourself from others.

I'm the little kid that is a part of who you really are. I'm going to keep affirming you for all your wonderful qualities. I will be speaking as if I am that special part of you who wants and needs to be loved and appreciated. I'll use affirmations and humor to keep you on the bright side of life.

ABOUT USING THIS BOOK

The Twelve Steps—A Guide for Adults with Attention Deficit Disorder is suitable for use in a ADD twelve-step support group meeting; with another person such as a sponsor, recovery partner, coach, or therapist; or alone. The book's intended and most effective use is within a group setting, where support, accountability, and fellowship can be shared with others. In a group setting, people have an opportunity to share their ADD-related stories and experiences, hear the stories and experiences of others, and come to realize that they aren't alone. This opportunity to share with others is a powerful healing tool for the ADD adult who has used isolation as a form of protection against others. Just knowing that others have similar symptoms, behaviors, and qualities is very reassuring and can offer relief from some of the anxiety and discomfort that often result from the ADD condition.

When using The Twelve Steps—A Guide for Adults with Attention Deficit Disorder in a group, it is suggested that one person act as the group facilitator. The facilitator assumes responsibility for the smooth operation of the meeting and makes the necessary arrangements. Although a different person will be chosen to lead the meeting each week, the facilitator will provide direction. It is the facilitator's responsibility to ensure that the group stays on target and observes guidelines for sharing. Suggestions and guidelines for facilitators are included in Appendix One.

The length of time required to complete the Step Study varies according to the needs of the group. Before beginning work on the Steps, it is helpful to spend two to three weeks on the material in the front of the book. The traits and positive qualities that are common in adults with ADD are covered briefly, and are discussed in greater detail in Step Four. The first week can include an overview of the introductory materials, the Twelve Steps, and the value of support and fellowship. The second and sometimes the third week can be devoted to reviewing the common symptoms, common traits, and positive qualities. It is suggested that one to two weeks be spent on each Step; possibly another week can be devoted to the Step review or the exercise in some of the Steps.

When this book is used in a group setting, it is recommended that small groups be formed with no more than six people. So if twenty-four people attend the meeting, divide them into four groups of six each. The small groups gather to discuss material and to share with each other for a portion of the meeting. Keeping the groups small provides ample time for each person to share. These groups work together for part of the meeting, and then gather with the large group for general sharing.

Step Study participation is an important way of breaking out of the isolation often experienced by adults with ADD. Using the Steps as the central tool, along with the support of the group, makes it possible to express long-suppressed shame, anger, and grief. The process involves releasing and letting go of the past. It makes room for the "one day at a time" serenity and calmness that result from working the Steps.

Using this book with a sponsor, recovery partner, coach, or therapist offers an opportunity for one-on-one sharing. This sharing provides a sense of focus, which is always helpful for ADD adults. We recommend that a person who uses this book also attend twelve-step support group meetings. A key to successfully working the Steps is a commitment to attending meetings and becoming part of the twelve-step process by sharing with others. A major component of healing comes from sharing our stories and carrying the message to others who have ADD.

It is likely you will go through the Steps more than one time. The program is a lifelong process to be used regularly, in part or in whole. At some point you may want to consider participating in a group that uses *The Twelve Steps—A Key to Living with Attention Deficit Disorder,* a workbook that applies questions to the materials in this book.

ABOUT THE AUTHORS

Our individual stories have a special and unique connection. Each of us began our recovery in twelve-step programs and came together as friends through attendance at AA (Alcoholics Anonymous) and ACoA (Adult Children of Alcoholics) meetings. In the course of our journey, we were guided to share our experiences as adult children by publishing four titles that "carry the message" to others who are looking for a better way of life. We are excited to have the opportunity to continue our commitment to spread the message of the Twelve Steps by developing this book for adults with attention deficit disorder. We truly believe that the structure of the Twelve Steps can provide a spiritual foundation for recovery from this disorder.

Jerry's Story

I keep a personal journal, and—because I don't do well with blank pages—I made my own journal with specific questions to answer each day. One of the questions is "What's going on?" One day I looked back over several months of journals and realized that my answer was usually the same. I had answered the question by writing "insanity," "confusion," or "scattered thinking." When I realized how often these words appeared, I felt pretty depressed.

It's funny, because the day before I had this realization, my son got in trouble at school. His fifth grade teacher complained, "R.J. ought to know how to control himself by now. I was teaching an important lesson when he blurted out 'Did anybody notice my new haircut?' You really need to discipline him more at home." She's actually a very patient teacher, so I knew she had to be pretty frustrated to mention the incident. I knew what she was going through because I've been like R.J. my whole life. Thoughts of my son and his problems at school reminded me that I've struggled with scattered thinking, restlessness, and an inability to get a handle on life ever since I was a child.

When my son's problems arose, it brought back vivid memories of my past. I had been in a twelve-step program for seven years, and the Steps had helped me to overcome a prescription drug addiction and to deal with my co-dependency. I realized the one thing I hadn't gotten from the Steps was peace of mind. I had peace in my spirit and in my heart, but my mind was scattered most of the time. I went to the only one who I knew would help me—I prayed. I asked my Higher Power to help me understand, to show me how to deal with this new awareness of myself.

That same week a friend called and told me about being diagnosed with ADD. She wanted to make amends for her ADD-related behavior that may have offended me or affected our relationship. Then she went on to tell me about ADD, and sent me some books and materials about it. The more I read, the more shocked I became. I couldn't believe I was reading about myself—my life story in print! The symptoms, the behaviors, the stories—they all spoke to me directly. The materials helped me finally understand why I act and feel the way I do. I'm a person who believes strongly in the power of prayer, and this answered prayer was a very special one I will always remember.

Although I knew I had ADD, I took the time to see a counselor and receive an official diagnosis. The counselor I saw was another answer to prayer because not only was he a specialist in ADD diagnosis, he was also a recovering alcoholic who uses the Twelve Steps. Armed with the knowledge of my ADD, equipped with the tools of the Twelve Steps, encouraged by the support of others, and guided by my loving Higher Power, I am beginning to make more sense of my life. I know my ADD can't and won't miraculously disappear, but I am learning how to live with it and gain victory over the moods that used to derail me. Thanks to my experience with the Twelve Steps, I know that when God has control, my negative ADD traits will diminish and my positive ones will flourish. Miracles happen! I have proof!

Jaclyn's Story

This story is about my grandma (I call her Gaga) and how ADD affects her life. I am writing this story because lately I have been spending a lot of time with her while she's writing this book. I'm 14 years old, and have enjoyed spending quality time with her ever since I can remember. Knowing I was going to visit Gaga was always something that would make my day pass by quickly.

My cousin Amber and I used to visit her at the same time. The three of us always had a bunch of laughs and acted crazy. I never really looked at my grandmother's behavior as being related to ADD. We would walk through the shopping malls and other places and have a blast. It was always strange to me that a sixty-year-old woman like my grandma could have so much energy. She had more than my cousin and I put together. We liked to tease her about it and called her the "energizer rabbit." She always seemed so excited and restless, even when everyone else was calm. She can't stand to do just one thing at a time.

I remember riding with her in the car—she would be driving, talking on the phone, writing down information, and looking through her purse—all at the same time! This was scary to me because I didn't think she could drive safely while doing a bunch of other things. Amber and I would always tell her to watch the road and pay more attention, but she didn't listen. We would just stare at Gaga in astonishment and wonder how she could do four things at once. Speaking of driving, she *constantly* went over the speed limit. She drove so fast that it felt like I was on an airplane.

Gaga is really good at changing the subject. We can be talking about school work, and somehow she starts talking about potatoes in Idaho. Also, when I talk to her, it doesn't always seem like she is paying attention. I'll ask her what color the sky is, and she'll say "Yes." She can't seem to hold still. Every time I look at her she's moving—either bouncing her feet, tapping on something, picking her fingers, or looking for something she thinks she lost.

Going to the San Diego Charger football games is one of the special things I get to do with Gaga. She has a bunch of season tickets, and takes my cousins and me to the games with her. We have a great time. She brings lots of munchies, and we have tailgate parties before the game. Charger games seem to help my grandma; she enjoys them, and they keep her attention. She drifts off occasionally, but she does really well at the games. I help her by saying "Poof!" when she gets distracted or starts picking her fingers.

Gaga thinks she's really cool because she has ADD. One day I told her that having ADD is no big deal. She turned to me in her usual "stuck-up and retarded" way and said, "Jaclyn, you work hard to get all A's on your report card, but I worked hard for my A's too. I drank to get my AA degree, I had alcoholic parents that earned me my ACoA degree, and I had to be labeled as lazy, stupid, and crazy to get my ADD degree. So how's that for an 'A' student!"

Luke's Story

Being in recovery from addiction, I owe my existence to God's grace and healing love expressed through the encouragement and support of many friends in recovery. What is surprising to me is how many of my close friends on the journey have been diagnosed with ADD.

It may be that my childhood environment prepared me for adult relationships with people who are easily distracted, constantly fidgeting, and who thrive on change, excitement, and chaos. I spent most of my childhood trying to survive in a chaotic, unpredictable, and often violent alcoholic environment. Early in my youth I abandoned the Sunday school notion that God listened to children's prayers. Unfortunately, I carried the legacy of addiction with me. Adult life became a battle for survival—one filled with broken dreams, lost expectations, and casualties. I suffered the consequences of failed businesses and marriages, and stress-related illnesses.

My twelve-step recovery began with ACoA (Adult Children of Alcoholics) meetings. I gravitated to leadership roles in the recovery community, and was instrumental in building an ACoA network in San Diego. It was here that I met Tracey.

When I needed to get things done, she was the person I relied on. We became involved in a publishing venture that provided twelve-step materials to people from addictive homes. We have been business partners and close friends for almost ten years, and continue to "carry the message to others" through continued use of the Twelve Steps as a tool for living.

Her recent ADD diagnosis answered many questions about her behavior that were a source of frustration for me, and that interfered with our ability to work together. For most of our working relationship, I found it extremely difficult to work in the same office with her. Her desk was usually piled high with a multitude of projects, all going on at the same time. She could answer questions from the staff, grab the phone on the second ring (she doesn't like to keep people waiting), and not lose track of what she was doing. Her ability to hyperfocus, together with her high energy and creative abilities, has been a major contributor to our success—as friends and as business partners.

I believe Tracey's Higher Power takes special care of her, or she couldn't have accomplished all she has. She was blessed with nurturing and devoted parents who provided her with structure and continually affirmed her for her abilities. She also spent twelve years in parochial school, where the need for structure and discipline were strongly emphasized. Since her diagnosis, we have been able to discuss our problems openly, and make compromises that benefit both of us. We joke about the craziness that is part of being in a relationship with an ADD adult. When it gets really bad, we have a clue—I say "Ssst!" and she knows that her ADD is getting in our way.

I have a close relationship with her son Charles, who also has ADD, and is very bright and talented. He struggles with low self-esteem, worries excessively, and tends to procrastinate. He owns a small manufacturing business, and is usually managing by crisis. Since he was diagnosed with ADD and began taking medication, I've found him more confident and less inclined to worry. He has a coach and is learning to operate in a way that helps him and his employees.

I continually make adjustments to meet life's challenges. With the help of the Twelve Steps and my recovery program, my childhood coping skills are serving me well. I can see the same thing happening to my friends with ADD. They don't lack for talent or resources, and since being diagnosed with ADD, they are adjusting their behavior to improve the quality of their lives. Both Tracey and Charles are in twelve-step programs, and I strongly believe this is making their journey easier.

About ADD

Attention deficit disorder is a neurological condition that is usually genetically transmitted, and is present in individuals from birth. It cannot be acquired as one grows older—but it does evolve over time. The symptoms may appear at different times, but the condition is always present. These symptoms make it difficult for the sufferer to function effectively in everyday affairs.

ADD is characterized by distractibility, impulsivity, and restlessness. People with ADD are easily distracted, have a low tolerance for boredom, and are very impatient. They have difficulty paying attention, are seriously disorganized, and tend to tune out of conversations. Many adults with ADD are attracted to situations involving high stimulation, and engage in risk-taking activities. Others are the quiet type who are more inclined to daydream, move slowly, or be underactive.

It is estimated that 3 percent of the adult population has ADD. This estimate derives from the theory that 70 percent of children with ADD continue to have the symptoms as adults. The symptoms rarely disappear completely, but they often diminish in adulthood because of compensating behaviors that people learn as they mature. This is especially true in women, because their symptoms are more often a result of hypoactivity, rather than hyperactivity. They are quieter and tend to prefer daydreaming and a quiet lifestyle. Men, on the other hand, are more often hyperactive, and the symptoms are not easily disguised.

ADD has existed as long as children have been around. Their overactive and unpredictable behavior was often labeled as "bad." These children were often described as wayward, impossible, incorrigible, or lazy. Treatment was discipline in the form of spanking, restriction, or shaming. Throughout history, these ADD children were the battered ones who nobody wanted to have around.

During the early years of this century, the behavior of these children was finally recognized as a medical condition rather than an act of disobedience or wickedness. In 1902 Dr. George Frederic Still, a British pediatrician, described some children in his practice as being difficult to control, showing signs of lawlessness and recklessness. He saw them as obstreperous, dishonest, and willful. He believed that the condition did not result from bad parenting, but was either biologically inherited or due to brain damage at birth.

In 1934, Eugene Kahn and Louis H. Cohen published *Organic Drivenness* which asserted that there was a biological cause for the hyperactive, impulse-ridden, morally immature behavior of the people they were seeing who had been hit by the encephalitis epidemic of 1917–18. This epidemic left some victims chronically immobile and others chronically insomniac, with impaired attention, impaired regulation of activity, and poor impulse control. The characteristics plaguing this group were what we now take to be the diagnostic triad of ADD symptoms: distractibility, impulsivity, and restlessness. Kahn and Cohen were the first to provide an elegant description of the relationship between an organic disease and the symptoms of ADD.

In 1937, Dr. Charles Bradley experimented with "wild kids" who were hospitalized for bad behavior. He gave them Benzedrine, a stimulant, and achieved remarkable results. This was a great moment for pharmacology. The medication altered neurotransmitters, and the children were able to remain focused. They actually calmed down and did not act out so uncontrollably.

During the 1960s, it became more apparent that the syndrome was somehow due to genetically based malfunctioning of biological systems rather than to bad parenting or bad behavior. By the early seventies, the definition of the syndrome included distractibility and impulsivity, and it was agreed that the condition ran in families. It was also known that the symptoms were often improved by the use of stimulant medication. In 1970, Dr. Virginia Douglas discovered that children with this condition were unable to pay attention, and the condition was labeled attention deficit disorder.

In the seventies and eighties, sufficient evidence was produced to determine that the problems inherent in people with ADD are related to their brain chemistry. Decreased blood flow causes them to get lost, lose things, and have difficulty understanding the "big picture."

One of the most recent studies was conducted by Alan Zametkin in 1990; it confirmed that adults with ADD have a different brain chemistry from those without ADD. The brain in a person with ADD uses less glucose, especially in the frontal region that governs attention, impulsivity, and distractibility. This results in less energy consumption, and inhibits the person's ability to keep impulses in check, plan and anticipate, and initiate behavior.

Research on ADD continues to bring new discoveries and help to people with ADD. The recent emphasis on adults with ADD makes it easier for sufferers to understand the disorder and get relief from the symptoms that have plagued them for most of their lives.

ABOUT THE TWELVE STEPS

Bill Wilson and Dr. Bob Holbrook, co-founders of Alcoholics Anonymous, developed an easily understood program that provides spiritual direction for managing and coping with life. Their process of recovery centers around the Twelve Steps, which they developed to improve the quality of their lives and to spread the message to other alcoholics. Unlike other self-help programs, the Twelve Steps represent a spiritual discipline that does not depend on self-reliance, determination, and human resources. The twelve-step program, as used by Alcoholics Anonymous, maps a course toward spirituality and faith, and offers a guideline for achieving peace and serenity in one's life.

The developers of the Twelve Steps discovered that their particular problems and needs were beyond the help of science, medicine, self-will, discipline, and human effort. Only by gathering together and sharing their stories with other alcoholics could they maintain sobriety and function effectively. They realized that their basic problem was a power shortage—an absence of power to overcome alcoholism. They came to believe that they needed a Power greater than themselves in order to have stability and sanity in their lives. They needed the resources of their Higher Power, the loving God of their understanding.

Richard's Story

I remember vividly the last time I attended a self-help seminar, where the retreat speaker scolded and pointed his finger like a pistol at the audience. The fireplace roared and crackled and cried out for my attention, but I was distracted by the fidgeting man next to me. I knew the man was as scatter-brained as I was when I watched him try to fix his name tag. He put the name tag on his knee, then frisked himself for a pen while scanning the audience. The name tag blew away, he dropped on all fours to look for it, then dropped his pen. I gave him my pen—for which he didn't bother to say thanks—and he proceeded to scribble the name *Richard* on the tag.

With Richard settled down, I turned my attention back to the speaker, who was saying "Pick yourself up by your bootstraps! Put your heart into it and try harder!" I knew the words well. I hear them inside my head every day—over and over. I even wondered why I was there. I already had a low enough opinion of myself, and didn't need a high-powered speaker to confirm my beliefs.

Richard's reaction was much stronger than mine. He began shaking his head and mumbling profanity. I nudged him and said, "Come on, we're outta here!"

Once outside, Richard exploded. "I can't do what that guy says—I can't do anything anymore!" He stopped talking and began crying.

I looked him and said, "I understand. I can't do it either."

With glasses off and handkerchief covering his face Richard said, "No, you *don't* understand. I bought a gun today to kill myself, but I decided to come here and give myself one more chance. I'm nothing but a phony. I can't stop cocaine, my wife hates me, I'm overwhelmed at work, and drowning in debt. I'm either in a state of panic or lost in depression, and my life sucks! No matter what I do, I can't figure a way out."

We stood silent for a moment, and I realized how Richard's behavior mirrored my own. His restlessness, distractibility, and poor self-image made me wonder if he also had ADD. I took a risk and told him about my recent introduction to a twelve-step support group for adults with ADD.

"Richard, I spent most of my life feeling and behaving like you do. I felt I had failed God, myself, and everybody else. I grew up believing that God helps those who help themselves, but I never could figure out *how* to help myself. Since attending twelve-step meetings, I've learned that what God *really* does is help those who *cannot* help themselves."

I'm still a newcomer to the Twelve Steps, but what I shared seemed to get Richard's attention. I told him about the serenity I found, and my new sense of worth since I admitted my need for help. I shared with him my renewed belief in a loving and accepting Higher Power who is doing for me what I could not do for myself.

When we parted, I knew I had a new friend. And I felt that Richard had found new hope—hope that he could find strength and courage from a loving God and from the people he would meet in twelve-step meetings.

The Twelve Steps help us make a much-needed change in the management of our lives. They connect us to wisdom, power, love, and order, through belief in a Power greater than ourselves. We allow God, who created order and harmony in nature and the universe, to bring order and sanity to our lives. Many of us exhaust ourselves trying to manage our ADD, control the unpleasant symptoms, feel good about ourselves, and survive in a world made for more "normal" people. In many cases, our control and "self-will-run-riot" mentality created new and more troubling problems such as addictions, co-dependency, poor health, depression, fear, and anger.

Twelve-step recovery is not sponsored by any religious group or entity—it has no official religious affiliation. It is a program that helps us to rediscover and deepen the spiritual part of ourselves that often becomes obscure. We also realize through working the Steps that our spirituality is an important part of the healing process. We learn to live our lives according to the guidance of our Higher Power. We realize that the void or despair we feel result from ignoring or rejecting our relationship with our Higher Power.

The foundation for this book is the twelve-step process. This process has helped countless millions of people recover from many forms of addictive, compulsive, or obsessive behavior. It brings together the tested wisdom and the proven effectiveness of the Twelve Steps. The material encourages self-understanding and emphasizes the importance of relying upon a Power greater than ourselves.

When used as intended, the Steps are a powerful process for allowing God to heal us. *The Twelve Steps—A Key to Living with ADD* is a spiritual tool that helps us regain balance and order, and leads us to improved health and increased happiness through a renewed relationship with our Higher Power.

Here are the Twelve Steps as they apply to adults with attention deficit disorder:

1. We admitted we were powerless over ADD—that our lives had become unmanageable.

Although it happens differently to each of us, there comes a moment of clarity when we recognize that our ADD symptoms are interfering with the quality of our lives. In spite of our attempts to control our lives and heal ourselves, we finally see that our lives are not working, and we quit fighting and stop playing God. We admit our powerlessness and the unmanageability of our lives.

2. Came to believe that a Power greater than ourselves could restore us to sanity.

We set aside our distorted image of God as someone who judges us and punishes us for our behavior. By admitting the fact that we are powerless, we receive a small seed of faith that enables us to believe in a Power greater than ourselves. We recognize that relying on our own power is not working, and that faith and believing is a gift we receive, not something we accomplish.

3. Made a decision to turn our will and our lives over to the care of God as we understood God.

We put our belief into action and admit our need for a new pilot. We assess our needs, abilities, and potential, and contemplate the required changes. We turn the controls over to God and trust that we will achieve serenity, sanity, and success, and begin to experience life as others do.

4. Made a searching and fearless moral inventory of ourselves.

We take an inventory of our lives, similar to a business inventory. We walk through the storerooms of our lives and make a list of our common traits and positive qualities. We look at our relationships and take stock of our resentments and fears. We note the shelves that hold our fears, feelings of worthlessness, and inappropriate behavior. We also find the compassion, creativity, and courage that we have because of our ADD. We ask for help from our Higher Power, who knows the contents of our warehouse far better than we do.

5. Admitted to God, to ourselves, and to another human being the exact nature of our wrongs.

This Step requires humility, and honesty. We share the results of our inventory with God, ourselves, and another human being. This isn't easy for adults with ADD. Our thoughts, feelings, and behaviors have become a part of who we are, and we are not always proud of our actions. To share our inventory with another person can be embarrassing and painful. If we reveal ourselves honestly and don't hold back the more shameful experiences, the relief we feel can have a powerful effect on us, and give us a great sense of freedom.

6. Were entirely ready to have God remove all these defects of character.

We examine our willingness to allow our Higher Power to bring changes into our lives. For most of our lives, we relied on our character defects, using them as tools to help us survive with ADD. The more willing we are to face our dilemma, the more easily we will remember the pain and wounds that our fear, manipulation, resentment, and addictions have caused us. Ultimately, we become entirely ready for God's help in removing some of our inappropriate and harmful behavior.

7. Humbly asked God to remove our shortcomings.

We use prayer as a way to humble ourselves and ask God to remove our shortcomings—one defect at a time. This is the time we talk seriously to our Higher Power in a very personal way about our inventory. In Step Seven we learn to draw nearer to God, knowing that God can help us focus more on our positive traits.

8. Made a list of all persons we had harmed, and became willing to make amends to them all.

We see how our ADD survival tools hurt others, and we recognize some of the harm we caused. We make a list of those we have harmed and prepare to make amends for our past wrongs. It is important to put ourselves on the list and look at the damage done to our self-esteem, our career, and our physical well-being.

9. Made direct amends to such people wherever possible, except when to do so would injure them or others.

We review the list we made in Step Eight and make personal or indirect contact with those on our list. We approach those we can with gentleness and understanding. Some situations will require a face-to-face meeting, and other situations will be handled by a change in our behavior. Making personal amends to ourselves is a vitally important part of Step Nine.

10. Continued to take personal inventory and when we were wrong promptly admitted it.

Step Ten involves a daily summary of Steps Four through Nine—a review of our thoughts, feelings, and actions. We admit what we find and ask our Higher Power for help in altering our behavior. In areas where we have harmed ourselves or others, we make the necessary amends. This is the beginning of our Step maintenance, where we continually monitor our behavior, and make corrections where appropriate.

11. Sought through prayer and meditation to improve our conscious contact with God as we understood God, praying only for knowledge of God's will for us and the power to carry that out.

Although the traditional forms of prayer and meditation are difficult for adults with ADD, they are key elements in maintaining peace and serenity. They offer a way to stay balanced and continue to rely on the strength of our Higher Power. God gives us the grace and freedom to pray and meditate in a way that fits our temperament. A thirty-second pause to say, "God, I need a clue" is sufficient, because God understands who we are and accepts us unconditionally.

12. Having had a spiritual awakening as the result of these Steps, we tried to carry this message to others, and to practice these principles in all our affairs.

Through working the Twelve Steps and surrendering to the process, we achieve a spiritual awakening that comes from abandoning self-will and embracing God's will. We voluntarily carry our message to others without telling them what to do. Instead, we share our own experience, strength, and hope by telling our own story. We apply these principles to every part of our lives and continue on our spiritual journey.

GOAL OF THE TWELVE STEPS

GOAL	PURPOSE	STEP
Peace with God	**Step One** is about recognizing our brokenness.	We admitted we were powerless over ADD—that our lives had become unmanageable.
	Step Two is about the birth of faith in us.	Came to believe that a Power greater than ourselves could restore us to sanity.
	Step Three involves a decision to let God be in charge of our lives.	Made a decision to turn our will and our lives over to the care of God as we understood God.
Peace with our-selves	**Step Four** involves self-examination.	Made a searching and fearless moral inventory of ourselves.
	Step Five is the discipline of admitting our wrongs.	Admitted to God, to ourselves, and to another human being the exact nature or our wrongs.
	Step Six is the beginning of an inner transformation some-times called repentance.	Were entirely ready to have God remove all these defects of character.
	Step Seven involves the trans-formation or purification of our character.	Humbly asked God to remove our shortcomings.
Peace with others	**Step Eight** involves examining our relationships and preparing to make amends.	Made a list of all persons we had harmed, and became willing to make amends to them all.
	Step Nine is the discipline of making amends.	Made direct amends to such people wherever possible, except when to do so would injure them or others.
	Step Ten is about maintaining progress in recovery.	Continued to take personal inventory and when we were wrong promptly admitted it.
Keeping the peace	**Step Eleven** involves the spiritual discipline of prayer and meditation.	Sought through prayer and meditation to improve our conscious contact with God as we understood God, praying only for knowledge of God's will for us and the power to carry that out.
	Step Twelve is about carrying the message to others.	Having had a spiritual awakening as the result of these Steps, we tried to carry this message to others, and to practice these principles in all our affairs.

ABOUT SUPPORT AND FELLOWSHIP

A vital component of recovery is being part of the twelve-step community. We need to interact with others who know what our lives are like and who can identify with our ADD-related struggles. People in twelve-step programs can relate to our pain and hear what we are saying without judging us or trying to fix us. We, in turn, can hear their stories and offer support. In recovery, we progress more quickly if we talk with others who can encourage us and support us as we try to change our behavior and improve our lifestyle.

The basic ingredient in the twelve-step program is the meeting, where people come together to share their experience, strength, and hope with others like themselves. In these meetings we find out we aren't unique—that many others share our symptoms, frustrations, and characteristics. We learn that we have many things in common—that together we can build a better understanding of ourselves and a better relationship with others. A twelve-step meeting differs from an ADD support group meeting in that it focuses on a spiritual approach to life. Reliance upon a Higher Power is the main focus and the key to success.

People in twelve-step support groups seem to create their own kind of energy and excitement. As people share their stories and re-create experiences, a sense of humor often emerges, and people feel comfortable laughing about some of the crazy things that happen. Especially effective and important in these meetings is the feeling of being connected that often comes when people share their stories. Feelings of isolation, not belonging, and loneliness often disappear as new friendships and understanding develop.

A side effect of attending meetings is an introduction to the value of discipline for people with ADD. The "rules" usually require that a person listens to the speaker, does not interrupt, and waits patiently for his or her turn. In addition, respect is asked for when someone is sharing. For someone with ADD, this means not speaking out of turn, having to sit still, and paying attention. In an inconspicuous way, this discipline paves the way for the behavior modification that adults with ADD so desperately want and need.

Also important in the twelve-step community is support and encouragement from a sponsor. A sponsor is someone who has experience in working the Twelve Steps, and has been in the program long enough to understand its principles and be able to help newcomers get a good start. When starting the journey, it is extremely valuable to find someone whom we can relate to, and with whom we feel safe enough to share our innermost thoughts and feelings. Experience suggests that it is more helpful for men to sponsor men, and women to sponsor women. Fundamentally, sponsorship is about friendship.

A sponsor does not offer advice—a sponsor shares his or her experience, strength, and hope. A sponsor is someone to call or meet whenever we need help or encouragement—someone who will be there anytime, anywhere. We can learn a lot from a sponsor by simply listening to the wisdom he or she has gained from the Twelve Steps, the guidance of a Higher Power, and the support of others in recovery. A good sponsor can help us to think about what we are doing and encourage us to use the tools of the program to find answers. But sponsors do not perform magic, resolve difficulties, make decisions for us, or accept responsibility for what we do. A sponsor understands the priority that recovery has to have in our life, and may strongly suggest that we attend meetings regularly, study twelve-step program materials, ask questions when necessary, and be willing to work the Steps as far as we are able.

Because using the Twelve Steps as a way to manage life with ADD is a new practice, it may be difficult to find a sponsor who is familiar enough with the Steps as they apply to ADD. If this happens, one can choose a recovery partner. A recovery partner is usually a peer—someone on our same level who can serve as a fellow traveler on the journey. A recovery partner can provide mutual accountability and support in the same way that a sponsor can, even though he or she may lack a strong background in the Steps. A recovery partner, like a sponsor, needs to be available whenever we need help.

Similar to a sponsor or a recovery partner is a professional coach. Having a coach is not a part of the twelve-step process, but it can be an effective tool for treatment. Coaching and its benefits are discussed in Appendix Two. Information about coaching organizations that provide support and encouragement on a professional level is also included in Appendix Two.

Many adults with ADD have behaviors that, although related to ADD, need to be dealt with in different ways. If we were accustomed to self-medicating and have problems with addictive behavior as a result of this, support is available in other twelve-step programs. We may be addicted to alcohol, drugs, gambling, food, or sex; or we may be co-dependent or an adult child of an alcoholic. If so, help is available in twelve-step groups such as Alcoholics Anonymous, Narcotics Anonymous, Gamblers Anonymous, Overeaters Anonymous, or Sexaholics Anonymous. Other twelve-step groups include Co-dependents Anonymous and Adult Children of Alcoholics. These groups can address particular needs and provide the support needed to gain freedom from these problems. Appendix Two includes a list of support groups.

The Twelve Steps—A Guide for Adults with Attention Deficit Disorder focuses on the principles embodied in the Twelve Steps and how the Steps can benefit adults with ADD. Other effective resources for recovery and treatment in the psychological and medical communities are also helpful and necessary. They are mentioned briefly in the text, often through the wisdom of the *Doctor* or the *Coach*.

Common Symptoms

Attention deficit disorder, no matter how mild or severe, has a tremendous impact on who we are and how we behave. It affects every area of our lives, and strongly influences our performance. If we were not properly diagnosed with ADD as children, our symptoms were often misunderstood. Our parents and others—even those closest to us—accused us of being everything from mischievous to malicious, from willful to wicked, from demented to demonic, from rebellious to reckless. The truth is, we had a disorder over which we had no control, and we were powerless over the behaviors which others mistook as willful acts.

For most of our lives these symptoms made us feel like square pegs in round holes. We sensed that we didn't fit, and strongly believed that we weren't normal. Others could sit still in class, listen politely, or patiently endure. But no matter how hard we tried, we simply could not do those things.

Bruce's Story

Bruce, an adult with ADD, looks back with horror at the nightmare of Navy boot camp. "I spent most of my time," Bruce recalls, "wearing out the asphalt around the parade field, becoming personally acquainted with and responsible for every toilet on base, and developing an arm strength possible only to those who have done more than a zillion push-ups. While everyone else had time to relax, catch up on sleep, or write letters, I was paying the price for my restlessness and impulsiveness, or else I was off somewhere daydreaming."

We all have stories about how ADD causes us to be misunderstood. Now, with the gifts of discovery and recovery, we can face and accept our symptoms for what they really are—manifestations of a disorder over which we have no control.

The primary symptoms that most commonly appear in adults with ADD are listed below. This list will help you recognize your own personal struggle with ADD, and the effect it has had on your life. The examples will help you identify some of the thoughts, feelings, and behaviors that you experience. You will not identify with all the symptoms, so respond only to the ones that apply to you.

We are easily distracted, and have difficulty paying attention. We have a tendency to tune out or drift away.

It is a struggle for me to stay focused or centered. When I least expect it, my brain changes channels, and I respond to the beat of another drum.

Although I can hyperfocus at times, I am more often distracted, and have difficulty staying on target.

At times I feel scattered and confused, like iron shavings attracted by competing magnetic fields.

I set out to clean the kitchen, and often find myself reading a cookbook and deciding to try a new recipe. I eventually finish the kitchen, but it takes me a while.

We are impulsive, and make hasty decisions without considering the consequences.

I make plans without consulting my family, then wonder why they don't share my enthusiasm.

I jump to conclusions before analyzing all the facts. This creates problems in my personal and business life.

I make decisions, commitments, purchases, even major life changes without adequately considering the consequences.

I buy things I don't need, then wonder where all my money went. The worst part is having to justify my actions.

We are restless, often hyperactive, and full of nervous energy.

I usually feel edgy and am always "on the go." My insides are constantly churning.

- I drum my fingers, twist my hair, pace, shift positions while seated, or leave the room frequently. I'm always looking for a way to release my excess energy.
- I channel surf with the television remote control, and find it hard to relax.
- I am an aggressive driver, and love to weave in and out of traffic. My favorite game is looking for "hole shots," and creating my own car race.

We have a strong sense of underachievement, and always feel that we fail to live up to our potential.

- Whether I am highly accomplished or floundering, I feel incapable of realizing my true potential.
- I feel like a failure and view success as something that only others achieve.
- In spite of my accomplishments and a satisfying relationship, I find it difficult to feel happy and fulfilled.
- In school I was called an underachiever, and that message still affects me today. I tend to be critical of my performance, even if others compliment me for a job well done.

We have difficulty in relationships.

- My inability to stay focused in the present moment gives others the impression that I don't care.
- I get bored easily, and have a hard time listening to what others tell me.
- I feel uncomfortable in group activities where social interaction is required. I prefer not to be noticed, because I'm afraid I will say the wrong thing.
- Sometimes I forget to say hello or goodbye, and others accuse me of being rude.

We are procrastinators, and have trouble getting started or feeling motivated.

- I put things off until the last minute, but the last-minute adrenalin rush makes the task possible, more interesting and stimulating.

▨ I use deadlines as a way to create panic and chaos. This enables me to hyperfocus, so I can complete the task on time.

▨ I allow piles of work to accumulate because I can't get organized. Only in times of hyperfocus can I actually get something accomplished.

▨ I'm inclined to start a project the night before it is due, stay up all night to finish it, and be totally burned out the next day.

We cannot tolerate boredom, and are always looking for something to do.

▨ I become bored with activities, conversations, and situations that do not interest me.

▨ I'm always looking for highly stimulating activities that keep my adrenalin flowing.

▨ When I sense boredom approaching, I look for something new and stimulating, rather than accept the idea of being bored.

▨ All of my waking moments need to be filled with something to do or something to think about. I cannot risk the possibility of having nothing to do.

We have difficulty getting organized.

▨ I make organizational plans, to-do lists, schedules, and resolutions, but still end up with piles on my desk, missed appointments, and unanswered phone calls.

▨ I have difficulty managing my time effectively. I am often late for meetings, and lose track of everything from keys to commitments.

▨ I often feel out of control and confused because I don't know how to organize my time and activities. My kids do a better job of organizing than I do.

▨ I do better when others remind me of appointments and give me direction and structure.

We are impatient, and have a low tolerance for frustration.

▨ I become impatient when things don't happen fast enough for me. I have a tendency to withdraw or react in anger.

▓ I like to know the bottom line without having to listen to all the details that I consider unimportant.

▓ If a line is held up because of coupons, price checks, or check cashing, I get impatient and want to lash out at the person creating the delay.

▓ I don't like waiting for people or dealing with people's problems.

We have mood swings with periods of anxiety, depression, or loneliness.

▓ Periods of depression affect my work, relationships, and perception of reality. I sometimes withdraw and isolate myself.

▓ A simple setback can bring on feelings of overwhelming hopelessness for me.

▓ My moods are unpredictable and can cause me to be either verbally and physically active or quiet and inactive.

▓ In the midst of a seemingly endless stream of thoughts, a memory of past failure or loss can submerge my mood instantly.

We worry excessively, and often have a sense of impending doom.

▓ Within minutes after awakening or arriving at work, I seem to search my mind for a topic to worry about.

▓ I use worry as a way to stay focused. It works like a cut on my finger—all my attention can be in one place.

▓ A feeling of impending doom seems to hover over me.

▓ I worry constantly about my health. I fear that I'm too fat, too thin, or have some fatal or debilitating disease.

We have trouble going through established channels or following proper procedure.

▓ I am a maverick at heart and do not like to follow rules or go through proper channels to complete a task.

▓ I tend to be critical of those in charge, and prefer being free to do things my way.

▓ I feel smothered by procedures, policies, and being directed by others. Needing to conform stifles my productivity.

▦ I have a hard time teaching my children to respect authority and follow the rules, because I have a hard time doing those things myself.

We have many projects going simultaneously, and have trouble following through with a project or task.

▦ I assume responsibility for more projects than I can realistically accomplish.

▦ I lose interest quickly and have difficulty completing one task before starting a new one.

▦ I prefer simple tasks that I can complete before I get an urge to start another one.

▦ I am capable of juggling lots of projects or commitments at the same time, but it creates anxiety and pressure for me.

We are poor observers of ourselves, and are often unaware of our effect on others.

▦ I have difficulty discerning how others perceive me. I rarely pick up the signals that indicate how well I am being received or if I'm talking too much.

▦ I tend to monopolize a conversation without knowing it. My friends tell me I talk too much about myself and don't give them a chance to share their story.

▦ I often exaggerate a story to make my point, and don't notice that others don't believe me.

▦ At work, I think others agree with me. In reality, they are confused by my "idea-a-minute" mentality.

We tend to say what comes to mind without considering the timing or appropriateness of the remark.

▦ I blurt out inappropriate comments without considering the possible consequences. Later, when I take time to reflect on what I said, I beat myself up for saying something so stupid.

▦ I have a hard time waiting my turn in conversations, and interrupt others while they are talking.

▦ I speak out of turn in meetings. This makes people angry, and I often lose the main point of the meeting, or lose the respect of those present.

▦ I have a reputation for making one-liner comments that hurt people's feelings.

We have a tendency toward addictive behavior, and use mood-altering substances to medicate ourselves.

▦ I use cocaine to help me focus, alcohol or marijuana to calm me down, and food to comfort me.

▦ I take prescription drugs as a way to speed up or slow down, depending on my needs of the moment.

▦ I use coffee and cigarettes to keep me energized, and to numb my feelings.

▦ I use work to give me focus, motivation, and a sense of accomplishment. At times, I use it as a way to avoid boredom.

We have difficulty in the workplace. We either change jobs frequently or have trouble getting along with our co-workers.

▦ I become bored with a job and cannot convince myself to stay, even though my financial security is at stake.

▦ I assume too much responsibility or take on too many tasks, then cannot fulfill my obligations.

▦ I change my mind frequently and create confusion among my co-workers.

▦ I waste time and resources on insignificant projects and spend time on things that keep my interest but have little value to the overall scheme of things.

We have a family history of ADD or other disorders of impulse control or mood.

▦ I have biological family members with strong evidence of ADD or other disorders of impulse control. I can trace ADD symptoms back several generations.

▦ I have family members who are considered high-strung and who have unstable careers.

▦ A lot of my close relatives have trouble controlling their temper.

▦ I have biological children with ADD and learned of my own ADD through their diagnosis.

COMMON TRAITS

As a result of our ADD, we develop certain character traits and behaviors that help us to live with our condition. Many of these traits and behaviors are developed in childhood as coping mechanisms, and stay with us through adulthood. They become a part of who we are and govern how we function. They are identified below as common traits among adults with ADD. Not all of the traits will apply to you. The list is intended only as a guideline for identifying those traits and behaviors that you have developed. These traits will be discussed further in Step Four as part of the inventory.

- We have feelings of low self-esteem that cause us to judge ourselves without mercy.
- We are fearful, anxious, and insecure in many areas of our lives.
- We do not give proper attention to our physical well-being.
- We have sudden outbursts of anger, often with loss of control.
- We are resentful, and blame others for our problems and struggles.
- We are either irresponsible or overly responsible.
- We are perfectionists, and put undue pressure on ourselves to perform.
- We can be indifferent, and demonstrate an "I don't care" attitude.
- We use rebellion and defiance as a way to disguise the ADD traits that make us feel "different" from others.
- We are defensive and respond poorly to personal criticism or teasing.
- We have difficulty in sexual relationships; we use sex as a source of high stimulation, or we consider sex uninteresting or a bothersome distraction.

- We have a compelling need for excitement and high stimulation in our lives.
- We use co-dependent and caretaking behavior to feel better about ourselves and avoid abandonment or rejection.
- We use denial as a survival tool to protect ourselves from reality.
- We use manipulation and control to manage our lives and make our ADD symptoms more tolerable.
- We tend to isolate ourselves and feel uncomfortable around other people.
- We have a strong desire to escape from the ADD characteristics that negatively affect us.

POSITIVE QUALITIES

Having attention deficit disorder can be rewarding and beneficial in many ways. When we learn to use some of the symptoms to our advantage, positive results follow. Our creative abilities are an indication of "impulsivity gone wild"; our restless and hyperactive nature gives us our "always-on-the-go" reputation. Many adults with ADD are successful entrepreneurs or gifted writers. As we learn more about our condition, and see where we can develop skills as a result of our ADD, new opportunities will open up for us. Eventually, our positive qualities can become a part of who we are, and contribute greatly to our success.

The positive qualities most often recognized in adults with ADD are listed below. Not all of them will apply to you. The list is intended only as a guide for identifying those qualities that you were born with or have developed. These traits will be discussed further in Step Four as part of the inventory.

- We are intelligent, and highly motivated by intellectual challenges.
- We are creative and highly imaginative, and can express ourselves in unique ways.
- We have high energy and meet challenges with enthusiasm.
- We are intuitive and can easily sense the needs and feelings of others.
- We are resourceful, and can devise ways and means to accomplish things.
- We are warmhearted and enjoy doing things for others.
- We are humorous and have an ability to make others laugh.
- We are hardworking, and have a never-say-die approach to life.
- We are willing to take risks, and see risk-taking as a form of excitement.
- We are loyal, honest, and trustworthy.

- We are flexible, and adapt easily to change.
- We are change agents, and like the intrigue involved in change.
- We are good observers and are able to find quick solutions to complicated situations.
- We are productive and effective if we like what we are doing.
- We are forgiving, and rarely hold grudges.

1

UNDERSTANDING STEP ONE

Being lost or disoriented is frightening and humbling. But even experienced hunters have become hopelessly lost in the woods. The best drivers have taken a wrong turn and become disoriented in a big city. Most of us have lost our car in a large parking lot or structure. In those times of confusion, we look for help. We call for other hunters. We pull into a gas station and ask for directions. We find a security guard to drive us around looking for our car. In Step One we also admit that we're lost. Our best efforts and attempts at living life on our own have left us confused and disoriented. We admit that we need somebody else's help.

WORKING STEP ONE

Step One is an opportunity to face reality and admit that our life isn't working. We embrace our powerlessness and stop pretending that we can fix everything. In a sense, we stop the juggling act that we have performed for so long. We admit that we can't continue the illusion of control. If this means that all the balls fall to the ground, then so be it. We are so tired of juggling our lives that we are ready to accept whatever comes.

PREPARING FOR STEP ONE

The way we try to manage our own lives brings us to the end of our rope. We've gone down the ladder as far as we can and have finally hit bottom. Our crazy ways and futile efforts have failed us, and we are ready to admit defeat. At this point, Step One provides the needed direction for our unmanageability. We prepare ourselves by realizing that Step One is a key element in the journey toward wholeness. This Step stops us. It puts a halt to our own efforts at managing our lives and gives us permission to quit.

STEP ONE

We admitted we were powerless over ADD—that our lives had become unmanageable.

By surrendering to powerlessness, I gain the presence of mind to stop wasting my time and energy trying to change and control that which I cannot change and control. This gives me permission to stop trying to do the impossible and focus on what is possible: being who I am, loving myself, feeling what I feel, and doing what I want to do with my life. —MELODY BEATTIE

Step One is the beginning of our recovery and an end to the craziness we feel as a result of trying to manage our condition by self-will alone. Step One gives us an opportunity to face reality and admit that life isn't working for us. With or without medication, we still have the same symptoms that have plagued us for most of our lives. At this point, we need help to adjust our behavior and make sense of our lives. Many of us are sick and tired of "doing what we don't want to do, and not doing what we want to do." When we get to this point, we can finally realize that we are powerless over our condition, and that our lives are unmanageable.

Jane's Story

This is my first twelve-step meeting. I'm not convinced I belong here, even though my doctor thinks it will help me. I've always believed I can handle this ADD thing. I read books, take medication, see a counselor, and do all the "right things."

But the truth is, I still feel as though my life is out of control. The medicine doesn't have the same effect it did in the beginning, and I really haven't changed that much. I still feel like it's all up to me, and I'm sure not much help to myself.

I feel like I've screwed up my whole life. I can't even accomplish the simple things like cleaning my house or fixing meals. I start off with good intentions in one part of the house, then POOF!—I'm off doing something irrelevant like reading old love letters or magazines. I do the same thing at work. No wonder I've been "let go" so many times.

All my life I've been called lazy or scatterbrained, and it's true. When others notice me, I'm usually off somewhere else, either daydreaming or not paying attention. My dad used to make fun of me and say to people, "Don't mind Jane. The lights are on, but nobody's home." With all that's going on in my life, I decided it couldn't hurt to give my doctor's suggestion a try. I know he's been in a twelve-step program for a long time, and life seems to work for him. When he explained powerlessness and unmanageability to me, it seemed as though he had climbed into my head and described me. Even though he was telling me his own story, I could really relate. I have to believe this is a good sign, and I'm excited about the possibility of the meetings helping me too.

Remember, you're not alone! There are lots of others who struggle with ADD. It is estimated that about 15 million Americans have it. Some pretty famous people may have had ADD. Albert Einstein didn't speak until he was four, and didn't read until he was seven. His teachers said he was "mentally slow, unsociable, and adrift forever in his foolish dreams." He was expelled from school, and Zurich's polytechnic institute refused to admit him.

The idea that we are powerless can sound crazy, and be very difficult to accept. Our whole life has centered around trying to control and manage the behaviors that make our lives topsy-turvy. As children, we learned how to get around the roadblocks we encountered in school and society, and had an uncanny ability to find a back door when the front door was shut. Finding such a back door was often our only chance to maintain some semblance of order and normality. As adults, we continue the same pattern of behavior.

> There is a difference between the unmanageability mentioned in Step One and the unmanageability associated with ADD. In Step One we simply admit that we cannot manage our lives on our own—that we need outside help. The unmanageability associated with ADD can result from mental confusion, feelings of being overwhelmed, disorganization, pending deadlines, the demands of others, and a host of other problems.

For most of our lives we believed that we could do anything—that we could manage ourselves and our environment without any help. The thought of asking someone for help, or looking critically at our behavior was something we were unwilling to do. We honestly believed that we had a handle on things, and that we were managing our lives properly. We didn't seem to notice or care how others perceived us. We were so locked into having control that we couldn't see how "out of control" we appeared to others.

The idea that our lives are unmanageable is easier to understand and accept than the idea of being powerless. We know how unmanageable life is for us—that's why we look for outside escapes and take medication. We are painfully aware of not fitting in—of somehow being different. We're running out of reasons to blame others for the lost jobs, failed relationships, and broken dreams that continue to interfere with our lives and create stress. At this point, we're recognizing that the problems follow us, and it's time for us to take some corrective measures and try some different tactics.

Attention deficit disorder, and the low self-esteem it often causes, keeps us from accomplishing our goals and interacting well with others. We lose confidence in ourselves and in our abilities, and end up with a stressful life that gives us little or no satisfaction. The stress compounds our problems, intensifies our fears and insecurities, and creates a sense of panic. Some of us depend on mood-altering substances such as drugs, alcohol, or food to relieve our tension and hide from the pain. In more subtle ways, others of us bury ourselves in school activities, work, relationships, or addictive/compulsive behavior to help us focus and avoid boredom. Our lives are full of unwelcome behaviors and overwhelming emotions.

> *It is not unusual for adults with ADD to self-medicate. The drugs most commonly used are cocaine or amphetamines to provide better focus; and alcohol, marijuana, or tranquilizers to calm nerves. Food and sex are used as a form of comfort. Self-medicating behaviors can include risk-taking adventures such as parachute jumping or fast and reckless driving. The abuse of these substances or behaviors can create serious medical conditions and damaging social consequences that compound the problem.*

In order for Step One to work, we need to picture the reality of our lives and be willing to accept what we see. Psychologists call this insight; theologians call it revelation; twelve-steppers call it a moment of clarity. Whatever it's called, it means that the fog is lifted and we see the truth about ourselves and our needs. It means we admit that our lives are just one big roller-coaster ride, that they have become unmanageable, and that we need help.

Two key factors cloud our vision of reality: self-will with its self-reliance, and denial with its many tricks—blaming, minimizing, generalizing, dodging, etc. When these factors are removed, we are able to recognize the truth about our lives and admit that we need help. The surrender that Step One implies begins our spiritual search for help. In the same way that we sought medical or other professional help for our ADD and its symptoms, we now need to seek out spiritual direction. Working Step One helps us find a spiritual key to living with ADD.

Surrendering is not an easy thing to do. As part of growing up, we developed our very own set of survival skills and behaviors. We have come to rely on them to meet our basic needs. However, our efforts to "go it alone" and "take care of ourselves" have caused stress and anxiety. We ought to be relieved to let go of the controls, but we're not. It's hard to let go and trust that

> *Structure is a key factor for ADD adults in maintaining stability. Take time each day to prepare a to-do list. Keep the list as brief as possible, and refer to it during the day to maintain direction and focus. Remember to Keep It Short and Simple (KISS).*

things will work out if we aren't in control. Like a drowning man, we thrash the water and fight our rescuer. Rescue is possible only when we stop struggling and admit that we cannot save ourselves without outside help.

Our thoughts, feelings, and actions are a part of who we are, and learning to live with them effectively requires a sincere effort to make adjustments where necessary. The process of surrender and working Step One requires an ongoing commitment if we are to experience lasting change. If we make the commitment, the spiritual process of the Twelve Steps will take us from the state of panic that self-reliance brings to the peace and serenity that trust brings. We will grow to welcome surrender as a doorway to peace. The need to do everything on our own and to take care of ourselves will diminish greatly.

It isn't necessary to understand all of the Steps immediately, but it is important that we start telling the truth about our lives. It's okay to admit that life has stopped working for us. It's okay to admit our gnawing sense of failure and the feelings of worthlessness and stupidity. It's okay to acknowledge the scattered thinking and forgetfulness, the sudden outbursts of anger, the depression, and the sense of being overwhelmed. Admitting that we are powerless over these feelings and behaviors opens the door to the healing change we seek.

Many of us who are diagnosed with ADD often feel a sense of relief in just knowing that we have a condition over which we have no control. We find comfort in having a label that fits and in educating ourselves about the disorder. Some of us find relief with medication because it helps us to pay better attention and adjust more favorably to our situation. Others prefer not to use medication because it doesn't help enough, makes us too nervous, disturbs our sleep or appetite, or has other undesirable side effects. Yet through education, counseling, and the support of others with ADD, we learn ways to compensate for our symptoms. We see how important it is to build structure into our lives, and we find comfort and new ideas by sharing our stories with other ADD adults.

God made me, and God doesn't make junk. I may feel low sometimes, but I know that God has a special plan for me—ADD and all. I just need to hang in there and discover the blessings that can come to me because of my positive ADD traits.

Despite our best intentions to live a happy and healthy life, we feel an emptiness deep inside—as if something is missing and we are somehow defective. Our lives may be better than they used to be, but we still feel like lonely orphans, like misfits who don't belong. We make a lot of adjustments just so we can "pass for normal." The dependence on medicine, the need to supervise our own recovery, the mind games we play to change our "cognitive-distortion," the costly counseling, the discipline to build structure and routine—all remind us every day that we are hurting. We often feel lonely, different, damaged, and inferior to others. No matter what people tell us, we still feel like square pegs in round holes. And all the time, the "negative tapes" play in our minds, telling us that we are stupid, worthless, lazy, and crazy.

The recognition that our lives are unmanageable as a result of trying to cope on our own can have a powerful healing effect. It frees us to see how crazy our lives really are, and how much energy we expend trying to behave like "normal" people. With this

> *Now that I know I have ADD, I'm going to do something about it. I know it won't be easy, but I'm worth all the effort it takes to recover.*

knowledge, we can begin our spiritual journey toward recovery by surrendering to the truth that we are not really in control. With the admittance of our powerlessness and unmanageability, we are ready to accept that a loving Power greater than ourselves can restore us to sanity.

> *When you are ready to admit your powerlessness over ADD, tell someone about it. The best place to share your experience of Step One is at a twelve-step ADD meeting. This is an important milestone, and you will gain a great deal of support and encouragement from the group.*

 # Key Ideas

Powerlessness: In Step One we discover that recovery begins with an admission that we are unable to change ourselves—we are powerless. We admit that, alone, we do not have the power to live life as God intends us to live it.

Unmanageability: We have tried to manage our lives, our ADD, and the lives of others. But our attempts continually meet with failure. In Step One we admit that we cannot control or manage our lives or the lives of others.

Passing for normal: ADD can make us feel like round pegs forced into square holes. Behaviors that are normal for people with ADD are often misunderstood by the "normal" people with whom we live and associate. For example, we can be misunderstood during a "normal" conversation. We easily forget a name, lose interest in a conversation, change the subject, or become restless and move around or fidget. We try hard to pass for normal by faking our way through life so we can feel that we fit in. We pretend that we are interested when we are really feeling bored, restless, impatient, or worthless. Inside we feel phony, and truly believe that we are not as good as others.

Negative tapes: The symptoms and behaviors that are part of the ADD syndrome have caused others to judge us. We were often ridiculed or punished for things we didn't even know we were doing. We unconsciously developed a set of negative messages that told us we were no good, lazy, inattentive, and less capable than others. These messages damaged our self-esteem. As we matured and entered adulthood, the negative tapes endured. Over time, we came to believe the messages, and now the voice on the tapes is our own.

Prayer for Step One

Higher Power, I'm tired of being in control.
I've tried to live life on my own for too long.
Today I feel as lost and confused as I ever have.
I've made a mess of things.
I don't think I can go on like this.
My mind is in a fog,
My heart is in pieces,
My stomach is in knots.
I cannot live life on my own,
And I don't want to anymore.
Higher Power, please hear this cry of powerlessness,
And come to me.
I can't find you on my own.

STEP ONE EXERCISE

A Time to Grieve

I sometimes hold it half a sin to put in words the grief
I feel; For words, like Nature, half reveal and
half conceal the Soul within.

—ALFRED LORD TENNYSON

Being diagnosed with ADD can trigger a lot of negative feelings. At first, we may be happy to have an explanation for many things about ourselves that we previously blamed on laziness, stupidity, or indifference. Eventually, reality sets in, and there is often a great deal of sadness and a sense of loss. We need to say goodbye to our old self-image, to some of our survival techniques, and begin a new way of functioning. Taking time to go through the grieving process is an important part of accepting our condition and letting go of the painful part of our past.

Dori Jean's Story

 I'll never forget the day I discovered that I have ADD. I was on my way to a Charger football game, and was listening to the audio tape *Driven to Distraction*. What I was hearing was my life story on tape, and I was beside myself with shock, anger, and sadness. I began to cry uncontrollably. By the time I got to the game and met my friends, I felt disoriented. I barely knew where I was or how I got there. It seemed as though I had detached from my body, and all awareness was gone.

At 60 years old, I discovered that I was born with a disorder which I cannot change or cure. Thanks to my involvement in a twelve-step program, I was able to surrender and admit defeat. I realized that I was about to embark on another journey of admitting my powerlessness and accepting my life as being unmanageable. Although I was relieved to have an explanation for a lot of my problems, I was unprepared for the shock. I spent the next four weeks grieving over the losses I had incurred as a result of my ADD behavior.

The grieving process that I experienced is included as part of this exercise, to serve as a guideline for your grief work.

Denial and isolation: My greatest denial was about my own behavior. I couldn't believe I was defective. I was proud of my hard-hitting, always-on-the-go nature. I thought that others respected me and my abilities. In reality, others saw me as power hungry and controlling.

As I learned more about ADD, I realized that this disorder had affected my entire life. I was able to see my life in a new perspective. I saw the harm I had done to myself, my family, and co-workers. I wanted to hide somewhere and escape the shame and embarrassment I felt. What others had always seen in me, I was just beginning to grasp.

Bargaining: My first inclination was to bargain with my family and friends. I wanted to ask them to give me a chance to change my ways. I believed that if I tried harder, I could be different. I hoped that my co-workers would trust me and work with me on projects without fearing that I would mess things up.

Anger and blaming: I felt very angry, and wanted to blame someone for my problem. I was angry that it took me so long to discover ADD. I was mad at my parents for not recognizing that I was different. I was angry at my husband for complaining about my sexual inadequacies. I was angry at my kids for telling me I was emotionally unavailable. I tried hard to believe that others were to blame for my problems.

Guilt: My guilt came from many directions. I felt guilty about the harm I'd caused, and the blame I'd placed on others who found me hard to live and work with. I felt guilty I didn't discover my ADD sooner and wasn't able to resolve it on my own.

Depression: My period of grieving involved a lot of sadness and feelings of hopelessness. I knew I couldn't change the past, and I was saddened by all I had lost. I felt responsible for my children's addictions, my son's suicide, my spouse's frustrations, and my co-workers' stress. I was depressed that my mother had needed to spend so much time with me as a child.

Acceptance: I am truly grateful for my twelve-step program. It has made it easier for me to accept my ADD. I learned about it by reading articles and books, and talking to others with ADD. After that, I obtained an official diagnosis, began therapy, and started attending ADD support-group meetings.

Grieving and coming to terms with a loss cannot remove the thoughts, memories, or pain of the misfortune, but it gives us a chance to process the loss and make peace with the past, and learn from our ADD-related losses. When we accept the losses, we find it easier to talk about them and share our grief with others.

Exactly how we express our losses does not matter. We can process our grief by talking with someone else, by writing letters or in a journal, or by expressing ourselves creatively through music, poetry, or painting. We will never be able to grow beyond the loss until we face it, feel it, and express it. If we refuse to admit the loss that we now silently harbor and hide, we face the risk of repeating its pain. We also risk missing the peace that comes with acceptance.

Select a loss for which you are in the process of grieving, or need to grieve. If possible, select a loss that is related to your ADD. The loss can include parental rejection, lost dreams or expectations, school-related losses, lost jobs or relationships, business setbacks, etc. Share your experience of grieving with another person. Express your feelings honestly and don't be afraid to express anger, guilt, or pain.

STEP ONE REVIEW

Step One forms the foundation for working the other Steps. Admitting our powerlessness and accepting the unmanageability of our lives is not easy. Although our behavior has caused us stress and pain, we find it hard to let go. The idea that our lives can work out well if we surrender control is a new concept for us. We prefer to feel that we have power and are in command.

❑ In what area of your life do you feel the strongest need to be in control?

❑ In what areas of your life do you feel powerless?

❑ What lost jobs, failed relationships, or broken dreams caused you to realize how unmanageable your life really is?

❑ How have you used mood-altering substances or behaviors to self-medicate your ADD symptoms? How do you feel about this?

UNDERSTANDING STEP TWO

"I looked at the turbulent waters and my legs turned to spaghetti at the thought of taking the inflated raft down the rapids—all in the name of fun. Then the river guide gave us instructions, taught us the commands, told us stories, and kept us laughing. He made the trip seem like child's play. He was so confident that I found my legs again, and knew everything would be fine. I trusted him to make this insane river ride a safe and enjoyable experience."

Step Two is about coming to believe and trusting in another to help us through turbulent and troubled waters. In admitting our powerlessness, we admit our need for guidance. Our Higher Power stands ready and willing to lead us through the waters ahead. All we need do is look beyond ourselves. God will provide the rest.

WORKING STEP TWO

When we admitted our powerlessness and the unmanageability of our lives, we planted a small seed of faith in our hearts. The act of surrender begins the process of coming to believe. We feel a growing confidence that someone greater than ourselves will take charge and help us find relief from our misery. In Step Two we acknowledge and nurture the seed of faith that grows from our surrender. This begins the process of trusting that a Power greater than ourselves is at work in our lives.

PREPARING FOR STEP TWO

We prepare for Step Two by setting aside our old images and mistaken beliefs about God. Many of us think that God doesn't care how we feel. We may picture God as a cruel ogre waiting to judge us for every wrong. To progress with Step Two we must be prepared to suspend our distortions of God and embrace the truth that God loves us and wants what is best for us.

STEP TWO

Came to believe that a Power greater than ourselves could restore us to sanity.

We found that as soon as we were able to lay aside prejudice and express even a willingness to believe in a Power greater than ourselves, we commenced to get results, even though it was impossible for any of us to fully define or comprehend that Power. . . .
—ALCOHOLICS ANONYMOUS (THIRD EDITION, PAGE 46)

Step Two takes us from powerlessness and unmanageability to trust. With the help of our Higher Power, we will experience a growing confidence and peace. We will come to believe that a Power greater than ourselves is capable of taking care of us and healing us. No religious training, knowledge of theology, or concept of God is required. To experience this belief, we need only a willingness to accept the truth and to respond to the faith our Higher Power puts in our hearts. This connection will grow and become a vital part of our daily lives.

> In twelve-step programs we say: "We who have done so little with so much now find that with faith we can do anything with nothing."

Steve's Story

Whoever was coming up the stairs wasn't in a hurry. The steady bang and scuff of each step echoed up the old church stairway. A man finally entered the room—dirty jeans, leather jacket, and greasy hair. He set a coffee cup down, walked to the other end of the fellowship hall, picked up a sugar packet, then headed back to his seat.

When seated, he quickly raised his hand and began talking. "I'm Steve. I have ADD, and I'm an alcoholic. I want to share how grateful I am to be here. These meetings are the only place where I feel welcome and loved. And you people showed me God when I had given up on God.

"I was sent away to a religious boarding school when I was a kid. Dad thought the sisters could handle me. He was wrong. Every sister, every teacher was the same. I learned from them that I was some special kind of sinner, and that God would punish me for my irreverence, fidgeting, outbursts, and anger. I once got hit so hard with the edge of a yardstick that I lost a tooth. I called my dad, and he said he'd knock all my teeth out if I got expelled.

"Then Sister Mary Ruth came to the school. It was the best thing that ever happened to me. She told me that I wasn't the piece of garbage I thought I was. And to prove it, she hugged me. I was totally embarrassed! Said she didn't hug garbage. In fact, she said somebody had to be pretty special to get a Sister Mary Ruth hug.

"I got lots of hugs and understanding from Sister Mary Ruth. She told me that God loved me, and she made me feel like I was somebody. She took time to help me understand the lessons and to catch up with the others. I believed her, and began to feel really good about myself.

"Then the bubble burst. I knew she was only telling me things to humor me. If God cared, how could he take her away? The other sisters said it was God's will that she got so sick. They said God needed her in heaven. If that was God's will . . . I sure didn't want anything more to do with God.

"I started to ditch school and get into a lot of trouble. After years of trying to kill the pain and myself, I found you people. I almost left the first time when I heard the word *God* in those Steps. You told me God loved me. You made me feel like I wasn't the piece of crap I believed I was. I even got a hug here that night.

"I'm still not sure about God. But I am sure about you, and people like you in these meetings. I really believe that you're there for me and that you accept me for who I am."

> The diagnosis of ADD can bring with it an abundance of opportunities for change and growth. One of your greatest sources for growth is education. As you learn about ADD, you will discover creative ways to live and excel. You will find many positive things about yourself. The important thing is to cling to the positive—and watch positive things happen.

Our surrender in Step One opened the door to the power of believing. Until we gave up on our ideas about how to run our lives, we couldn't believe that another way could be better. Change actually begins with surrender, because without it, we can't see alternative ways of doing things. Contrary to what many people believe, *surrender* is a positive word. It is when we learn the art of surrender that new opportunities present themselves. Like the general who knows when to surrender in order to gain a better position, we also need to learn that to surrender is to open the door to new opportunities.

Step Two is about believing. It is a state of mind we must have before we can start anything. If we don't believe in something, it probably won't happen. The idea that we "can't do it" will support our low self-esteem and prevent us from being promoted. On the other hand, if we believe we can earn the promotion, our attitude and performance could very likely earn us the promotion.

Belief is a powerful force. It is the place where we begin, before anything can happen. Some of us have trouble believing, because we want more proof—more assurance. As adults with ADD, we want to know the bottom line before we begin, or we tend to let worry and anxiety get in our way. But that stops us from being able to believe. Thomas Edison, who had ADD, did not know what he was going to discover when he did his experiments—he only believed. He intuitively knew he was onto something, but did not know what it was. Undoubtedly, his ADD traits motivated him to take the risk and keep searching for that unknown something that he knew was there.

> *Creating structure and building trust are key elements in reducing ADD-related chaos. Communicate daily with a trusted friend, coach, or your sponsor. Share your goals and projects, as well as your fears, feelings, and your current mood. This will help keep you centered and in good spirits. It will also give you a greater chance for order and stability.*

For many of us, this Step presents a major obstacle because it requires believing and trusting in someone besides ourselves. We find it hard to trust others; we feel more secure if we keep a safe distance from them. We've relied on our own resources and learned to survive by either acting like Mr. Tough Guy or Little Miss Helpless. We believed that if others knew who we really were and how stupid and inadequate we felt, they would reject us. Unless we let go of our distrust and begin to lean on God, we will continue to function in this insane manner.

> In order to experience the power of believing, you need to interact with others. Try joining a twelve-step ADD support group where you can hear about others' experiences and speak the truth about yourself. You will see how their willingness to believe in a Power greater than themselves has opened the doors to new opportunities. For many people, willingness to trust begins with finding an accepting, loving group of people who understand their needs, problems, and fears.

Depending on our religious background, we all formed some understanding of God. Some of us believed that God was an authority to be feared—not a loving Higher Power. As children, we were anxious and fearful of being punished for behavior we couldn't control. We were scolded for daydreaming, being restless, or causing trouble in school and at home. Our fear of displeasing God magnified our growing sense of shame and worthlessness, and supported our belief that we were bad and enjoyed causing trouble.

Some of us harbor anger and resentment toward God. We might believe God cursed us with attention deficit disorder and didn't give us the proper tools to overcome our troublesome traits and uncover our posistive qualities. Some of us reject God because belief and trust in God didn't relieve our pain, stop the abuse, or cure our ADD. We may even doubt that God exists because of the way we were constantly shamed and ridiculed. Whatever the reasons for our struggle to trust God, the key to resolving the struggle lies in honestly facing our doubts and disappointments, and looking forward to enjoying a more sane existence.

Believing is an important spiritual principle—a spiritual tool. We have the power to use it, but we must act on that power. If we don't, it won't do us much good. If we say we believe in God, then continue to run our own lives, we are not truly believing. For some of us, belief in self-will and our ability to manage our own lives is all we have. We may perceive God as a crutch for children and weak-willed adults who are

> Shame is like a magic spell that others cast upon me to control me. It causes me to feel worthless and bad—that who I am is not okay. I can't change who I am, but I can learn to accept myself, warts and all. The Twelve Steps are helping me to reject my shame, and trust that my Higher Power loves me unconditionally.

incapable of managing their own lives. But as we begin to experience God's love and acceptance through the lives of others in recovery, we begin to see God's true nature.

One way God helps us to clearly see the chaos and insanity in our lives is to bring us into contact with others whose experiences resemble ours. As we share our stories in meetings and through fellowship, we learn how others cope with anxiety, worry, procrastination, and difficulties in social interaction. It can be comforting to tell others how frustrated we get when we start a project the night before it is due and then stay up most of the night to finish it. If we let our hair down, we may even laugh at the craziness of it all.

During the initial stages of accepting the presence of a Higher Power, it's helpful to make note of the special occurrences around us. We can view coincidences in our lives as small miracles, gifts, or simply interventions of our Higher Power. When boredom strikes, going for a walk and enjoying nature can give us a perspective of the miracle of nature, and at the same time contribute to our health and welfare. By thanking our

You can minimize boredom by listening to exercise tapes while biking, jogging, or using exercise machines. Team sports such as racquetball, basketball, or dance aerobics provide a great workout. For a real "adrenaline fix" and a chance to enjoy the fresh air, try roller-blading along the boardwalk.

Higher Power for simple things, like the unexpected check that comes when needed most or the traffic ticket we didn't get, we learn to recognize and accept our Higher Power's presence in our lives. Our willingness to express gratitude to this Power helps us come to believe.

The positive belief we develop in Step Two is an important building block in recovery. We have always had belief. But we may have believed untruths instead of the truth about ourselves or the ability of a loving Higher Power. We thought we could make it on our own, but at the same time, we believed the negative tapes that told us we were worthless and incapable. Our success depends heavily on the belief we place in the truth and in our Higher Power. The difficulty we have with positive believing is that we want something more certain before we begin.

> *I found a way to believe in a Power greater than myself by talking to my dog. I pretend that she is my Higher Power, and I go to her for comfort whenever I'm feeling lonely or when I need some special love and attention. I also hug her when I am really happy, and thank her for being my special pal. It's like she really hears me, and delivers my message to the Higher Power I can't see, touch, or feel.*

A common problem for adults with ADD is our need to see, touch, and feel in order to understand. It's helpful to select something with which we identify. For example, a pet can offer comfort, companionship, and unconditional love and thereby remind us of our Higher Power. The night sky, with its limitless expanse and brilliant stars, can serve as a chapel for nighttime meditation and connection with the creative God of the universe. People whom we respect for their spirituality might help us focus on our Higher Power. More traditional reminders like the Bible, church sanctuaries, or religious art might help us connect with a Higher Power.

 **Key Ideas**

Higher Power: Step One helped us understand our powerlessness. Now we need a Power greater than ourselves to help and heal us. Our Higher Power does not have to be precisely identified or named, or be anything like the God we were taught about in childhood. Our Higher Power, who will nurture and carry us through our recovery, will be revealed in divine power, presence, and help according to our unique needs.

Coming to believe: Coming to believe requires trust and commitment. It is one thing to believe that a chair will hold our weight; it's another thing to sit in it. When we sit in the chair, we truly believe in it. In Step Two we come to believe that a Power greater than ourselves can restore us to sanity. We begin to do more than acknowledge God's existence—we begin to exercise trust that God will hold us. This belief prepares us to make the decision in Step Three to turn our will and our lives over to God's care.

 Prayer for Step Two

I pray for an open mind
So I may come to believe
In a Power greater than myself.
I pray for humility
And the continued opportunity
To increase my faith.
I don't want to be crazy any more.

STEP TWO EXERCISE

Developing Self-Esteem
It is difficult to make a man miserable
while he feels he is worthy of himself and claims kindred
to the great God who made him.
—ABRAHAM LINCOLN

Distortions of Self-Esteem

Parents, teachers, and significant others who were ignorant or intolerant of our ADD often treated us in ways that hurt our self-esteem. We were treated as though our problem was a moral weakness and not a neurobiological disorder. We were told that we were not as fast or smart or capable as others. We were belittled, disciplined, or treated harshly because of our restlessness, inattentiveness, poor reading and handwriting skills, and whatever else we did that others believed was inappropriate.

A number of unkind, humiliating words were used by others to shame, motivate, or characterize us. It is important that we recall these words and see how they contributed to our distorted thinking about who and what we are. As we remember what others called us, we will realize that these descriptions became a part of the vocabulary we used to describe ourselves.

Circle the words others used to describe your behavior or attitudes when you were growing up. Add words that you remember being called.

stupid	loser	cheater
daydreamer	fake	restless
fidgety	liar	lazy
selfish	foolish	hypervigilant
rude	absent-minded	worthless

crazy	reckless	mean
mischievous	destructive	sloppy

_____	_____	_____
_____	_____	_____
_____	_____	_____

In time, we came to believe we were what the descriptive words implied. We saw ourselves as others had labeled us. The poor self-image that resulted was more damaging and destructive than anyone could have known. The seemingly harmless labels that others gave us seeped into our hearts and poisoned our self-esteem and sense of worth. As adults, many of us are plagued with feelings of worthlessness and self-hatred. Our minds mercilessly harangue and condemn us with self-inflicted disapproval. We tell ourselves how rotten, disorganized, stupid, and inadequate we are. And we often get caught in moods of self-condemnation that pull us down like a whirlpool.

Components of Self-Esteem

We can use simple techniques such as calling a friend or going on a bike ride to break self-condemning cycles and moods, and to feel temporary relief. The deeper work of improving our self-esteem is more difficult, but it's possible. The first step is to identify how you were denied the basic components of self-esteem. As you read the components of self-esteem, think how these basic esteem-building needs were frustrated or unmet in your life.

Acceptance (denied): "I don't belong."

We felt unwanted as a child because our ADD behavior created difficulties for our caregivers. Constant criticism made us feel like an unwelcome nuisance.

Significance (denied): "I'm not important."

We believed we were unimportant because those close to us found it easier to ignore us. They tolerated us better when we were not seen or heard. Others didn't seem to have time to spend with us.

Competence (denied): "I can't do anything."

It was hard for us to perform as well as others in such things as handwriting, reading, paying attention, and cleaning our rooms. We developed the belief that we couldn't do anything.

Virtue (denied): "I can't do it right."

During childhood we were treated as though our problem was a moral weakness and not a neurobiological disorder. Our sense of virtue was denied when we were called disobedient, rebellious, deceptive, or manipulative.

Power (denied): "I can't make it happen."

Our caregivers treated us in ways that made us feel helpless and incapable of responding properly to our environment. Such things as abuse, ridicule, threats, punishment, and anger caused us to feel powerless.

Once we identify the missing components, we can begin to develop them for ourselves. In recovery we derive these important components of self-esteem from supportive and nurturing relationships with others and from our Higher Power. Attending support-group meetings and getting acquainted with other adults who have ADD is a great way to develop self-esteem.

Acceptance: "I belong."

We associate with people or groups that give us a sense of acceptance and belonging.

Significance: "I am somebody."

We have key relationships in which we are made to feel important. We nurture healthy relationships with spouses, children, and friends so that our role in their lives can bring satisfaction and meaning.

Competence: "I can do something."

We use and develop our skills, talents, and abilities. We understand that, although we cannot do everything well, we are competent in the areas that are important to us.

Virtue: "I can do it right."

We find ways to demonstrate our responsibility, kindness, honesty, and integrity. We are learning that with God's help, we are able to develop godly character and virtue.

Power: "I can make it happen."

We recognize and acknowledge that we have power to accomplish God's will in our lives. We measure our power with a spiritual standard, not by the expectations others have placed upon us.

Developing Self-Esteem

The definition of *esteem* is "to have great regard for; value highly; respect." We have a saying in the program: "If you want high self-esteem, then do esteem-able things." Acts of kindness and consideration toward others are esteem-able things, and are often acknowledged by others as good deeds. When we accomplish projects or tasks in areas where we have talents and abilities, we feel good about ourselves. When we place ourselves in the company of good people, our esteem grows. When we continue to improve ourselves and strive to learn new things, we develop a higher regard for ourselves.

STEP TWO REVIEW

Step Two gives us new hope. We see that help is available if we simply reach out and accept what our Higher Power has to offer. In Step Two we begin to expand our spiritual life, which helps us become who we want to be. What is required of us is a willingness to believe that a Power greater than ourselves is waiting to help us. What follows as we progress through the Steps is a process that brings our Higher Power into our lives and enables us to grow in love, health, and grace.

❑ Explain your current understanding of your Higher Power. How do you interact with that Higher Power?

❑ List and explain any difficulties are you having in believing that a Power greater than yourself can help you to manage your affairs more effectively.

❑ How do your childhood memories of God influence your feelings today?

❑ Cite an example in your life where you believed strongly in something and experienced positive results because of your belief.

3

UNDERSTANDING STEP THREE

Imagine the insanity of trying to perform surgery on ourselves. At the first hint of pain from the scalpel, we would stop. Healing would never happen. It's equally insane to think that we can manage our own recovery. We must put our lives into the hands of our Higher Power, who knows about our disorder and the frustration it creates. Only our Higher Power has our best interest at heart and knows what we need for healing.

WORKING STEP THREE

Step Three involves making a decision and preparing for the Steps that follow. As in other big decisions, we must carefully consider the condition of our lives. We can better understand that condition by thinking about the way we tend to nurse an old car along. In spite of countless repairs, the breakdowns continue to occur. We finally realize the old car will continue to fall apart and cause us trouble, and we decide to buy a new car. In the same way, we think we can repair ourselves. But the reality is that we can't. No matter how much energy and time we spend, our "management by self-will" is bound to fail us. Our only solution lies in deciding to get a new manager.

PREPARING FOR STEP THREE

We prepare for Step Three by working Steps One and Two. We must be convinced that we are powerless and that our lives are unmanageable. When we have admitted this, the ability to believe will come naturally. Then all we need to do is recognize and respond to that belief. When the first two Steps are in place, Step Three comes easily.

STEP THREE

Made a decision to turn our will and our lives over to the care of God as we understood God.

Until a man has found God and been found by God, he begins at no beginning, he works to no end. He may have his friendships, his partial loyalties, his scraps of honor. But all these things fall into place, and life falls into place, only with God. —H. G. WELLS

Step Three embodies the central theme of all the Steps. It is the point at which we decide to turn our will and our lives over to the care of God as we understand God. It is an important cornerstone for building an effective and peaceful life. Steps One and Two established the basis for turning our lives over to God's care. Now, in Step Three, we make the actual decision to hand control over to our Higher Power. It would be great if a one-time decision settled the issue of who's in control, but Step Three, like the earlier Steps, is an ongoing process. We are accustomed to running our lives through self-will, and we are bound to slip up. In the process of working the Steps, we will repeat Step Three many times, often on a daily basis. Right now, we are just beginning to understand what it means to turn things over to our Higher Power. Repeated working of the first three Steps helps build a solid foundation for using the Steps as part of our lives—one day at a time.

Gwen and Vicki's Story

"Is she here today?" Gwen handed her purse to Vicki.

"Yeah. She's in the back." Vicki kneeled to tuck the bag under the counter. "Didn't you see her broomstick in the parking lot? Tell me, Gwen, how come it feels like she's always here? She owns two other stores, and I know she torments the other employees just as badly."

"Well, Vicki, it's probably that damned invention called the phone." Gwen winced as she swallowed a sip of cold coffee. "Yesterday, I thought I'd get a break because she was at the mall store all day. But she called me every five minutes to tell me something so stupid and insignificant that I didn't even bother to write it down. Anyway, I knew she'd forget the conversation ten minutes after she hung up. And when she's here, she's always 'touching base' with the other stores."

"I know," Vicki huffed. "It's like she doesn't think we can to do anything right. Plus she's always got some new idea. The problem is, we get stuck with all the work, trouble, and torment to make her ideas work. And just about the time we get the new display up or the new coupons made, she changes her damn mind and comes up with a new off-the-wall idea."

"I think she's a control freak," Gwen whispered as she looked back toward the office. "Or just plain mental. She's got to be involved in everything. I don't think she trusts anybody but herself."

"I don't know what her problem is, but I get nervous just being near her. She buzzes around here like a queen bee and makes impulsive decisions about the store and the employees. The bizarre part is that she thinks we're the ones who are crazy."

"You'd think she'd get a clue since she can't induce a manager or most clerks to stay longer than two months . . . Oh, I take that back! The last store manager lasted three months."

"Yeah, but she didn't speak English," Vicki laughed. "Shh! Here she comes."

I found out that lots of famous people had ADD, and they were very gifted. They had trouble getting along in the world just like I do. If they were able to overcome their difficulties, then I can too. I learned that:

- *Winston Churchill failed sixth grade.*
- *Thomas Edison's teacher said he was too stupid to learn anything.*
- *Isaac Newton did very poorly in grade school.*
- *An expert said of Vince Lombardi, "He possesses minimal football knowledge and lacks motivation."*

Many of us come to this program with a negative attitude about the world in which we live. We're tired of feeling inferior, tired of being ridiculed, and thoroughly fed up with the idea of trying to change who we are. Our attitude may be based on hurtful childhood experiences, unhappy school memories, or simply the accumulated difficulties of life with ADD. If we experienced abuse or injustice as children, we may find it hard to trust anyone, especially God. Whatever the source of our tainted perceptions of the world, our recovery will be hindered if we cannot let go of our resentments and fears, and surrender our lives to God. The principle and practice of Step Three is a leap of faith. We let go of our own control and make a decision to put our lives in God's hands. From there, in Step Four, we begin to take action.

As humans, we have basic, God-given instincts. These instincts move us to meet a number of important social, security, and sexual needs. Our social instinct moves us toward companionship and the recognition of others. Self-esteem, an important part of our social make-up, enables us to feel good about ourselves. Without self-esteem, we wouldn't cooperate and couldn't accomplish much. We also have security needs that include our material and emotional well-being. These needs motivate us to work and provide shelter and clothing for ourselves and our loved ones. Our sexual instinct creates in us the desire to reproduce and keeps the human race going.

These instincts often far exceed their proper functions. Our desires for sex, for material and emotional security, and for an important place in society often tyrannize us. When this happens, trouble results. As adults with ADD, our need to "do it our way" and control the outcome often causes us to make hasty decisions that hurt us and others. We allow our self-will to run riot and we end up feeling resentful, fearful, and stressful because our plan didn't work as we had hoped it would. We may also feel guilt, shame, or remorse because our attempts at self-gratification have hurt others.

> *Operating on self-will alone and needing to "do it our way" creates intense anxiety and stress. This can lead to unhealthy conditions such as high blood pressure, increased heart rate, muscle tension, poor digestion, and a host of other problems. On the other hand, learning to relax and trust the outcome will enable your body to function normally. It's like driving on the busy freeway or trusting another driver and riding in the back seat. Trust is healthy!*

All of nature is cared for and controlled by God-given instincts or laws. The goose can't decide to fly east instead of south, or west instead of north. A rock can't decide to fall up—it obeys gravity and drops. Humankind, on the other hand, has the freedom of choice. People can choose to live according to God's will, like the rest of nature, or people can choose to live life on their own. Living life on our own and apart from God's will is what Bill Wilson calls "self-will run riot." This distorted self-will is the major cause of our misery.

Many of us developed obsessive-compulsive behaviors as part of living life through self-will. These behaviors were a way to expel our excess energy, provide high stimulation, and keep us focused. We depended on these behaviors for protection and survival. They helped us live in a world where we knew we were somehow different from others. If we are to suc-

> *In recovery, it doesn't matter if you win or lose— it's how you play the game that counts. God cares more about your character than your reputation. Stop spending a lot of time trying to impress people with your "superhuman" abilities. Turn your reputation over to God, and focus on building your character.*

cessfully work Step Three and achieve some peace and serenity, we need to be willing to lay aside these traits and trust our Higher Power. For example, we may have tried to fool others and ourselves by always having multiple projects going at the same time. Juggling many projects helped us feel good about ourselves and caused others to think we were "superhuman." We felt better if others envied us for our special talents and energy. This bolstered our self-esteem and made us feel important.

Admitting responsibility for our self-defeating behavior is often very difficult. It implies that we are "bad" and reinforces our childhood beliefs about ourselves. So we use denial as a shield against facing ourselves as we really are. When denial is at work, it is like a shuttered window, closing out the sunlight—truth. In Step Three, we begin to open the shutters and allow our Higher Power's light to enter. With God's light and our emerging trust in God, we can examine our behavior and accept reality.

Step Three is an affirmative Step. We make a decision and commit to change. Thoughts of surrendering control of our lives may fill us with fear. Even though we see what "control" has done to us, we fear the loss of people or things vital to our lives, such as family, job, health, or sanity. Our lives may already include many relationships that are being hurt by our behavior. Rather than being discouraged by our discoveries, we can use them to prompt our surrender to a Power greater than ourselves. The guidance of our Higher Power will direct us to healing and restoration, not to further loss.

I've decided it's time to change the negative feelings and distorted images I have about myself, and start looking at my positive qualities. Although ADD has some negative aspects, it also provides me with a lot of special talents that other people don't have.

In Step Three, we acknowledge our need for guidance, and make the decision to surrender our lives to God's care. Our Higher Power becomes our new manager, and we accept life on God's terms. We discover a way to live that is free from the emotional pollution of our past, allowing us to enjoy new and wonderful experiences. Step Three provides us with an opportunity to turn away from behavior that fosters resentment, fear, guilt, addiction, discouragement, and sickness.

Step Three can liberate us from the tendency to worry excessively. Worry is a fact of life, and many of us use it unconsciously as a tool to obtain focus and to motivate ourselves. Worry is a form of pain, and pain is a powerful motivator and focusing tool. For example, if a part of our body hurts, all of our energy and attention is directed toward relieving that hurt. In the same way, we use worry as a way to center our attention. We wake up in the morning and scan the horizon for that one terrible, threatening thing that can overwhelm us with dread and concern. It's an unpleasant feeling, but suddenly we're up, moving, focused, and motivated. We're on our way . . . but with a knot in our gut.

If we wake up in the morning and look for God instead of something to worry about, we can put our focus on the first three Steps. We can admit our powerlessness over worry, believe that our Higher Power is able to help us through the day, and surrender the whole mess to God. We are still up and motivated, but our focus is on God's power rather than on our worries. We can then reap the benefit of peace. There is a paradox in the way this program works. The less we try to manage our own lives, the more effective we become. When we give up managing on our own and trust in our Higher Power's plan for us, we find we are calmer and more accepting of things around us. Friends may even compliment us on how well we are managing our lives.

Step Three may make us feel like we are losing our identity and everything that is important to us. Most of us have tried desperately to control our environment and what is going to happen. Many of our behaviors were developed during childhood as a way to control our ADD and protect ourselves from being mistreated by parents, teachers, and other important people. We tried hard to please others so they would love us and tell us we were okay. As adults, we tend to continue these behaviors to avoid rejection. Deep within us may be a fearful childhood memory and a trembling child anxious about someone's anger, criticism, threats, or violence.

> *Rather than spending a lot of time worrying about what you need to do, spend it on arranging your schedule so that you can accomplish your objectives for the day. Plan to reward yourself when you complete important tasks, stick to your "things to do" list, or reach an objective. A simple reward can be treating yourself to a hot fudge sundae or having lunch with a special friend.*

The conditions and circumstances in which we were raised often kept us from ever trusting in God. We rarely received encouragement that we could accomplish our goals

Consider using the twelve-step slogan "One day at a time" to relieve the tendency to worry excessively. Brooding over yesterday and fretting about tomorrow do not help the here and now. Remember, yesterday is history, tomorrow is a mystery, and today is a gift. That's why we call it the present!

and achieve our potential. Instead, pressure was put on us to sit still, pay attention, look alive, stop distracting others, or simply act normal. We may have believed that God had little or nothing to do with our lives. Our parents may have told us that the one we disappointed the most was God. Some of us felt that our prayers were not answered because we didn't please God. Step Three gives us an opportunity to experience our Higher Power's healing love and to start repairing the damage that has been done. With God's loving help, we can look forward to a return of childlike spontaneity and a growing capacity to give and receive love and nurturing.

Many of us begin Step Three by deciding to turn over only certain parts of our lives to God's care. We are willing to surrender the problem traits and behaviors that are making our lives unmanageable, troublesome, or stressful. Yet we cling to other traits and behaviors because we think we can manage them or because we believe they are necessary for our survival. We eventually realize that we cannot barter with God. We must be prepared to surrender our entire will and every part of our lives to our Higher Power's care if we want lasting help and change. When we are able to accept this fact, our journey to wholeness has truly begun.

Learning to trust in a Higher Power will enhance the quality of our lives. We will no longer feel the need to carry our burdens by ourselves. Our difficulty with relationships, both socially and at work, often caused us to isolate ourselves and keep a safe distance from others. As we surrender and learn to trust, we will begin to relate better with others and feel safer in social and work settings. With God's presence, our sense of self-esteem will improve, and we will begin to recognize that we are worthwhile human beings. Our capacity to receive and give love will increase, and we will come to place great value on fellowship and sharing with others.

> *Adults with attention deficit disorder need encouragement. Without it, they wither and never feel they can accomplish anything worthwhile. With encouragement, they light up and can achieve great things. As part of your recovery, it is important to surround yourself with people who will encourage and support you. It is also important to work on your relationship with God and find encouragement there.*

Key Ideas

Turn it over: This statement of surrender is the main theme of Step Three. Imagine turning over your car keys to someone else, or turning over a job or a responsibility to a more capable person. People who have been in the program for any length of time talk about turning over problems and daily troubles to their Higher Power. For those of us who are working Step Three for the first time, it helps to use imagery. Whatever imagery you choose, let the meaning always be the same: the surrender of your will and life to God's care.

Self-will: Self-will is the determination within us all to control our own lives. Self-will in itself is not wrong. God has given us the power to choose. Our whole trouble is the misuse of willpower. We try to resolve all our problems, gratify selfish desires, and control others through self-will alone. What we need to do is seek God's will for us, and use self-will to choose

God's plan. Relying on God's will in our lives brings us hope, healing, and peace. Our self-will is best exercised in choosing surrender to God.

 Prayer for Step Three

I surrender to you my entire life,
O God of my understanding.
I have made a mess of things
Trying to run it by myself.
You take it, the whole thing,
And run it for me,
According to your will and plan.

STEP THREE EXERCISE

The Worry Bears

Worry is interest paid on trouble before it falls due.
—W. R. INGE

The original root meaning of our English word *worry* is "to strangle or to choke." Although we don't usually interpret the word that way when we use it, worry does indeed choke our life. At least, that's how it feels.

Worry strangles us by stealing our joy and peace and by tormenting us with fearful anticipation of something that may not even happen. Worry causes us to borrow stress from tomorrow. Most worry comes from a perceived threat—not a real one. Nine times out of ten our worry turns out to be in vain. We got choked for nothing.

When we are faced with a real threat—for example, a bear in the woods—our bodies react to help us meet that immediate threat. A number of physiological changes prepare us to do one of two things: fight the bear or flee from it. To prepare us to fight or flee, our bodies pump adrenaline, increase the heart rate, increase blood pressure, constrict blood vessels, send blood from extremities to vital organs, stop digestion, stand hair on end, dilate pupils, and on and on.

After the fight with or flight from the bear, all these functions return to normal. When we suffer from chronic worry, anxiety, or stress, we meet the bear every day. Even though when we worry, the bear is only in our minds, we convince ourselves that the bear is a real threat waiting for us *all the time.*

We adults with ADD unconsciously use worry as a way to focus and motivate ourselves to get going. We scan the horizon with our first conscious thoughts of the day, searching for a reason to fret. Once we've found our worry of the day and convinced ourselves that there *really is* a bear, our bodies prepare us. We get tense, blood pressure rises, digestion stops, etc.

The problem is that an extended period of worry-related stress in our minds and bodies can make us truly sick. We become ill because the energy that should be used to keep us healthy is being wasted to prepare us to fight or flee from an imaginary bear that never leaves our minds. This can lead to heart attacks, strokes, ulcers, joint pain, and more.

We all live with a host of bears in our minds. There are Papa Bears, the big worries; Mama Bears, the medium worries; and Baby Bears, the small worries. These bears or worries are not always present in our minds; they pop in and out like guerrilla warfare commandos doing their damage and then disappearing. These worries change from time to time as we age or change situations in life.

A helpful exercise is to list these bears or worries. Naming them, getting them out in the open, and sharing them with another person can be very healing.

STEP THREE REVIEW

Step Three is an affirmative Step. It is time to make a decision. In Steps One and Two we became aware of our condition and accepted the idea of a Power greater than ourselves. Although we are beginning to know and trust God, we may find it difficult to allow a Higher Power to take charge of our lives. But if the alternative is facing the loss of something critical to our existence, we may find it easier to accept our Higher Power's guidance.

❑ Which parts of your life are you willing to turn over to your Higher Power?

❑ Which parts of your life are you unwilling to turn over to your Higher Power? What is your resistance to giving them up?

❑ In which area of your life do you experience the greatest sense of chaos and unpredictability? Explain.

❑ What do you hope to achieve as a result of your decision to turn your life over to God's care?

❑ In what ways do you use pain or worry to focus your attention?

UNDERSTANDING STEP FOUR

If we were blind, we would have a number of special needs. We would find it difficult to clean house and ask a friend to help us. This friend would see areas in need of cleaning and help us clean them. In Step Four we discover the areas of our lives that need attention, and start the process of internal housecleaning. Denial has blinded us to a lot of the dirt in our corners, and self-will has kept us from seeking help. In this Step, our Higher Power comes to us as a caring friend. God opens our eyes to our faults and helps us to see our positive qualities.

WORKING STEP FOUR

Just as a business takes inventory, we take inventory of our lives. With clipboard in hand, we walk down the aisles and note our resentments, fears, and harmful conduct. The inventory must be thorough, so we open the crates and look inside. We are either angry about something, afraid of something or someone, or ashamed or remorseful about something we have done. We look for guidance from our Higher Power, who knows the contents of our warehouse far better than we do.

PREPARING FOR STEP FOUR

Most of our lives we used self-will to cope with our ADD in ways that were defeating and damaging. We prepare for Step Four by accepting that we have a condition over which we have no control. The behaviors and traits that we will discover and face in this Step are the results of our attempts to control life on our own. Step Four is an emotionally demanding Step. It is important to take care of ourselves during and after the inventory process.

STEP FOUR

**Made a searching and fearless moral
inventory of ourselves.**

*Whether we're looking at resentments, fears, or harms done to others, the
roots are the same . . . But these weren't (in fact couldn't be) immediately
evident to us. We had to start from something we could see and work
backward to the truth."* —JOE MCQ, *THE STEPS WE TOOK*

In Step Three we made a decision to turn our will and our
lives over to God's care. In Step Four we look for the
behaviors and traits that hinder us. We examine our
behavior and expand our understanding of ourselves. We identify our defects so that we can discuss them in Step Five and
learn more about them. In Steps Six and Seven, we become
ready to let go of our shortcomings and ask God to remove
them. This journey of self-discovery forms an important foundation for our recovery and will require honesty and courage. It
will help us to remove the obstacles that prevent us from knowing the truth about ourselves and the will of God for our lives.

Dennis's Story

"The last thing I want to do, Dennis, is to hurt you. But a small company like ours can't afford to have
someone like you as an employee."
As Dennis heard the words, his eyes drifted to the
pictures, diplomas, and letters on the office wall.

> *Step Four is a demanding Step, and a lot of uncomfortable feelings and memories may surface. Try to be aware of your feelings, and invite support from a close friend, coach, or sponsor. Remember, it is only natural to be afraid of what you may uncover as you look closely at yourself and your behavior.*

"You don't take action on the work I give you. I find you helping other employees with their work, but you neglect your own. I can't rely on you, Dennis, and it doesn't even seem to bother you. There's no way I can help you if you won't help yourself."

"Am I fired?" Dennis asked. The boss nodded. "Okay then. Bye." And Dennis was gone. He couldn't bring himself to clean his desk. He didn't even stop to get his helmet before jumping on his motorcycle. He just had to ride! As the bike roared up the steep climb to Foothill Road, Dennis's mind exploded with memories.

Today's episode brought back memories of his father that were real enough to cause pain in his arm—the same pain he had felt every time his father had lifted him off the ground by one arm and scolded him. "Stop, Daddy! You'll break my arm!" Dennis spoke the words into the wind as if the scene was actually taking place.

"Maybe if I break your arm, you'll learn to slow down and think. You won't act like such a damn fool, and embarrass me. *I* never got kicked out school, and I sure don't want *my* son to be a bum and a loser."

Dennis's bike hugged each curve along Foothill Road. He lost himself to the speed, the narrow ribbon, the blind turns, the wind, and watery eyes. The thrill and excitement transported him away to a distant place where he felt safe. Then, with a jerk of his wrist, he surged forward with a new burst of speed to meet the next curve. But as he held the bike down to hold the curve, he saw Foothill Road straightening out ahead of him. The snaking and challenging adventure became a boring ride through the valley.

Like Dennis, many of us find ways to kill the pain. Dennis liked to use speed and the high-risk stimulation of a dangerous motorcycle ride to escape his feelings of low self-esteem. Others of us use alcohol or drugs to self-medicate, so we can kill the pain and control the craziness. Many of our traits, behaviors, and survival skills are not as apparent to us as they are to others—especially to those who love us. We developed them as a natural response to our environment. They are the unwelcome results of living with ADD. They define how we learned to cope, not who we are as people.

Denial is a key survival skill that we learned early in childhood. It stunted our emotional growth by keeping us in a make-believe world. We often fantasized that our situation was better than it really was. Denial protected us from our feelings and helped us repress our pain. Our shame and guilt caused us to be silent, rather than to be honest and to face the

> *I came into this world with ADD. I didn't do anything to cause it. My job now is to stop looking for ways to kill the pain and start identifying my good qualities. When I get rid of the negative tapes, I'll be able to replace them with positive ones and see the special person I really am.*

fear of being ridiculed by others. This withdrawal hindered us from developing into mature, emotionally healthy adults. As our self-discovery unfolds, we begin to recognize the role that denial plays in our lives. This realization is the basis for accepting the truth of our personal history.

Denial has many faces and can be easily masked. It appears in different ways and operates in various fashions. Some recognizable forms are:

Simple denial: To pretend that something doesn't exist when it really does (e.g., ignoring physical symptoms that indicate we are overextended, anxious, or stressed).

Minimizing: To acknowledge a problem but refuse to see its severity (e.g., admitting to making a poor decision, then ignoring its consequences).

Blaming: To recognize a problem, then blame someone else for its cause (e.g., blaming others for our troubles in the workplace).

Excusing: To offer alibis and other explanations for our behavior (e.g., calling in sick when the real reason for our absence is that we did not complete an assigned task on time).

Generalizing: To deal with problems on a general level and avoid personal and emotional involvement in the situation (e.g., sympathizing with a friend's problems, but not offering specific information that we believe could help).

Dodging: To change the subject and avoid threatening topics (e.g., talking about the weather when our spouse is trying to tell us that we don't listen and don't seem to care).

Attacking: To become angry and irritable as a way to avoid looking at our inappropriate behavior (e.g., lashing out at the boss when he is trying to offer constructive criticism).

> It's about time I stopped denying so many things about myself and looking for someone else to blame for my ADD. I read an article recently that shed new light on my condition. I have Another Darn Disorder that provides me with lots of special qualities. I am Actually Delightfully Driven, I'm learning to Avoid Daily Disorder, and my Attention is Definitely Directed. Not bad for someone with attention deficit disorder!

Step Four involves writing an inventory of our resentments, fears, and hurtful conduct. Resentments are manifestations of self-will that result from wrong judgments, and block us from God. We develop resentments because we feel a threat to our self-esteem, emotional well-being, security needs, relationships, or ambitions. The resentments dominate our lives and often cause us to allow people and things to control us. When we give people and things permission to dominate our lives, we cannot carry out the decision we made in Step Three to turn our will over to God's care.

Fear is a powerful and destructive force that cripples and disables many of us. Fear limits our ability to be rational and paralyzes our ability to take action. Fear dominates our minds and makes it difficult for us to see situations in their true perspective. Like resentment, fear is a result of self-will gone wrong. Fear arises from wrong beliefs. It often prevents us from expressing ourselves honestly and stops us from responding appropriately to threatening situations.

When motivated by self-will, we often make wrong judgments about people and things. Those judgments lead us to practice wrong beliefs, which become resentments and fears. Because of these resentments and fears, we take wrong actions that cause shame and remorse, and reinforce our feelings of low self-esteem. In many cases we act

> *Practice the twelve-step slogan "Live and Let Live," and you'll have fewer resentments and fears. The AA Big Book says, "We are careful never to show intolerance or hatred . . . We have stopped fighting anybody or anything. We have to!"*

out in inappropriate ways to kill the pain of our low self-esteem. So to change our behavior, we must first face and accept our resentments and fears. Then we need to acknowledge that self-will has caused us to make wrong judgments based on wrong beliefs.

Preparing our inventory requires that we look to God for guidance. We renewed our relationship with our Higher Power in Steps Two and Three, and now we ask God for help. We will look closely at our personal history and acknowledge what we see there. As the process unfolds, we will recognize the need for change. This task will be much easier if we remember that God is with us and will help us to courageously review our faults.

Step Four gives us the opportunity to recognize that certain skills acquired in childhood may be inappropriate in our adult lives. Blaming others for our misfortunes, denying responsibility for hurtful behavior, and resisting the truth are patterns we must discard. We learned these patterns early in life. As we look at these self-defeating behaviors now, we may feel troubled. Things we thought were forgotten may surface and bring back painful memories. Our willingness to be honest about what we uncover will give us the clarity of mind that is vital for our continued recovery.

In Step Four you are being asked to review your life and identify behaviors that are unhealthy for you. This can create a great deal of emotional pain and stress. It is sometimes possible to calm frazzled nerves without medicating yourself. Try a warm bath, soft music, a peaceful walk, or a massage. Take adequate vitamins, because your body uses more nutrients when you are under pressure.

Most of our negative thoughts come from resentments, fears, or harms done to others. The inventory involves looking at these areas and reviewing what we find. When completing the inventory, we list the resentments, fears, and harms done so we can analyze them. We want to see who was involved, what caused the problem, how it affected us, and what wrongs were done as a result of our behavior. A key to success in doing this is to look at each section separately. The first thing we do is list the people and things we resent, fear, or harmed. When this is done, we go to the next topic, which is what caused the problem. The next step involves how it affected us, and finally we list the "exact nature" of our wrongs.

Putting our thoughts on paper is valuable and necessary when completing Step Four. The process of writing focuses our wandering thoughts and allows us to concentrate on what is really happening. It often causes repressed feelings to surface and gives us a deeper understanding of ourselves and our behavior. Our fearless moral inventory provides insights about our behavior. Instead of judging ourselves, we need to accept whatever we discover, knowing that each discovery is merely another step toward a healthier life. We must be honest and thorough to complete Step Four successfully. With God's help and our personal courage, we can expect to receive limitless benefits.

The work we do in Step Four helps us to know and understand ourselves better. When we do this, we will have a clearer idea of why we respond the way we do. And we will have better control over the resentments and fears that create chaos in our lives. We will have a better understanding of who we are, where we're going, what we stand for, and what we want to do with our lives. If someone says something we don't like— something that might have hurt our feelings before—it won't hurt us so much now. We've learned a lot about ourselves, and we're not as vulnerable as we used to be.

> As an adult with ADD, it is natural for you to feel intimidated by the idea of having to make a written inventory. It is an important part of your healing journey, so try to make it a "project" that you organize, and set a deadline for completion. Do it honestly and thoroughly, and invite the support of your coach, therapist, or a close friend to help you schedule time to complete your inventory.

When preparing our inventory, we may encounter some difficulties, and find it hard to continue. If we are blocked at

> *Learning as much as possible about ADD can help you learn about yourself and make your inventory easier to complete. Read books and talk with others who have ADD to increase your understanding of the disorder. The more you know, the better equipped you will be to discern the difference between your character defects and the symptoms of ADD that you cannot change.*

some point, denial may be operating. Or we may be overcome by anxiety about the outcome of the inventory and what we are discovering. We should stop for a moment, reflect on what we are attempting to do, and analyze our feelings. In times like this God's presence is important, and we must be willing to ask for it. Without it, the journey will be a lot harder, and we may get discouraged.

Key Ideas

Moral inventory: A moral inventory is the process by which we learn the truth about ourselves. We examine our behavior and honestly face what we see. Our common traits and positive qualities represent our true selves. This inventory is for our benefit, and is something we prayerfully accomplish with God's help.

Survival skills: Survival skills are those familiar defenses that we developed to cope with our ADD and to protect ourselves from the pain we encountered in childhood. These early childhood survival skills followed us into adult life and added to our struggles.

Denial: Denial is a key survival skill that protects us from facing the fact that something is wrong. We ignore the real problems by replacing them with a host of elaborate explanations, rationalizations, and distractions such as minimizing, blaming, excusing, generalizing, dodging, attacking.

Resentment: Resentment is a major roadblock to recovery. It fills us with bitterness and anger toward those whom we perceive as threats to our security or well-being, or toward those who have caused us harm. If not removed, our resentments act as anchors that hold us down and prevent progress and growth.

Fear: Fear is often our first response to anything new that we don't understand. We meet change with fear because we feel threatened by so many things. Fear creates a physical response that begins with the release of adrenaline and ends up with our whole body on alert. This alerted state often leads to persistent and unwanted tension and can develop into stress-related illnesses.

 Prayer for Step Four

Dear God,
It is I who have made my life a mess.
I have done it, but I cannot undo it.
My mistakes are mine, and I will begin
A searching and fearless moral inventory.
I will write down my wrongs.
But I also will include that which is good.
I pray for the strength to complete the task.

Important Guidelines for Preparing Your Inventory

The inventory in Step Four has two parts: The first part of the inventory involves looking at the common traits and positive qualities that are common to adults with ADD. They are the tools you developed to cope with the symptoms of your disorder. These common traits may be harmful to you and to others, and may prevent you from achieving your true potential. They are the character defects that cause your self-esteem to be lower than it should be. The positive qualities are common to people with ADD, and can be learned. Examining your traits and qualities is an important part of the healing journey, and helps in assessing the changes you must make to have a more fulfilling life.

The second part involves looking at resentments, fears, and harmful conduct. Worksheets for your inventory of resentments, fears, and harmful conduct begin on page 104. For the best results, follow the instructions below when completing the worksheets.

Column 1: List the people, institutions, or principles you resent or fear. In the case of harmful conduct, list the people who were affected by your conduct. Include the childhood resentments, fears, or harmful conduct that still affect you. Complete column 1 from top to bottom before going to column 2.

Column 2: Ask yourself why you are resentful or fearful, or why you behaved the way you did. List what happened to cause the resentment, fear, or harmful conduct. Complete column 2 from top to bottom before going to column 3.

Column 3: List your needs or ambitions that were affected. These include social needs (e.g., self-esteem, relationships), security needs (e.g., material or emotional security), and sexual needs. Complete column 3 before going to column 4.

Column 4: List the nature of the wrongs, faults, mistakes, or shortcomings that surfaced because of your resentment, fear, or harmful conduct. For example, if you feel that your job (material security) was threatened because of a co-worker's criticisms, you might revert to anger, defiance, or disrespect. The "exact nature of your wrongs" will surface here, in preparation for Step Five. When all four columns are complete, review your list.

Finally: Read from left to right and determine for yourself the answers that emerge from your writing. This will prepare you for sharing the exact nature of your wrongs with God, yourself, and another person in Step Five. If your inventory has been honest, thorough, and balanced, a new sense of freedom awaits you.

Glossary of Terms for Column Four

Anger: Extreme displeasure, hostility, indignation, or exasperation toward someone or something; wrath; ire.

Co-dependency: Preoccupation with and extreme dependence on a person or object.

Defiance: Disposition to resist; willingness to contend or fight.

Dishonesty: Deceit; disposition to defraud; justifying behaviors by explaining ourselves dishonestly.

Disrespect: Lack of respect or reverence; discourteousness; inconsiderateness.

Envy: Jealousy; longing for an advantage or benefit enjoyed by another; desire to possess the same benefit.

Impatience: Restlessness or shortness of temper, especially under irritation, delay, or opposition.

Impulsivity: Hasty, needless action; acting momentarily.

Irresponsibility: Unreliability; disrespect for higher authority.

Lust: Lechery; an intense indulgence in inappropriate sexual activity; above-normal desire.

Manipulation: Use of artful or unfair means to control or play upon others.

Selfishness: Greed; hoarding; never having enough of anything.

STEP FOUR EXERCISES

Common Traits
Realizing who you are is your own choice.
—ALEX REYES

This exercise will help you identify with the common behavior traits and survival skills that many adults with ADD report. You will not identify with every one. But for those with which you do, make note of how they apply to you.

We have feelings of low self-esteem that cause us to judge ourselves without mercy.

▥ Years of criticism, failure, and punishment for "bad" behavior have left me feeling defective and inferior to others.

▥ I feel horrible inside, as if having ADD means there is something wrong with me.

▥ I am ashamed of and humiliated by my poor reading and handwriting skills.

▥ I think of myself as a "screw-up," undeserving of praise and incapable of success.

We are fearful, anxious, and insecure in many areas of our lives.

▥ I spend a lot of my waking hours in a state of panic and anxiety.

▥ I worry about what others think of me, and often conclude that they don't like me.

▥ I feel insecure when I talk to my boss, or when I have to confront those close to me.

▥ I have fears of failure, poverty, abandonment, and a host of other unidentified, unseen, and unrealistic dangers.

We do not give proper attention to our physical well-being.

▦ I have chronic muscle tension; neck, back, and shoulder pain; and symptoms of arthritis.

▦ I am susceptible to allergies, and have trouble with hay fever, asthma, headaches, and a tickle in my throat.

▦ Unless I am seriously ill and cannot function, I don't allow myself to take time off and get well. I am more inclined to work while I am sick, and suffer the consequences.

▦ My anxiety and stress levels are always high.

We have sudden outbursts of anger, often with loss of control.

▦ I explode quickly, and cool down quickly. I get over my anger long before others get over their anger.

▦ I get angry at others when I think they are slow, incompetent, or stubborn.

▦ It frightens me when I lose control and become enraged for no good reason.

▦ I get angry at myself for allowing my ADD-related behavior to hurt me or those close to me.

We are resentful, and blame others for our problems and struggles.

▦ I resent the way people tease me about my behavior. I feel they don't understand, and have no right to ridicule me.

▦ When I think of the way I was treated as a child, I resent those who abused and punished me for behavior I couldn't control.

▦ My resentments often interfere with my personal and business relationships.

▦ I feel resentful when others do not include me in their plans. I immediately think that they don't like me, or that I have done something wrong.

We are either irresponsible . . .

▦ I tend to be irresponsible when I am asked to do something that does not interest me.

▨ I don't like the responsibility of having to do housework, and I wish that my family members would take a more active part in helping me.

▨ I sometimes feel like a victim and give up trying.

. . . or we are overly responsible.

▨ My need to make things happen quickly causes me to take on too much responsibility.

▨ In childhood, I assumed the role of responsible child, and am still the one who is called when family members have a problem.

▨ I make too many commitments, because I feel it is my responsibility to take care of whatever others ask me to do. I have difficulty saying No.

We are perfectionists, and put undue pressure on ourselves to perform.

▨ I have unrealistic expectations of myself and set unrealistic standards for my behavior.

▨ I am overly critical of my appearance. I'm always worried that I am too thin, too fat, or too ugly.

▨ I demand perfection from others, which discourages them from helping me.

▨ I strive hard to be "the best" at sports, work, parenting, housework, and whatever else I am doing.

We can be indifferent, and demonstrate an "I don't care" attitude.

▨ If someone hurts my feelings, I become indifferent and act as if it doesn't matter to me.

▨ Rather than look for satisfying employment and risk disappointment, I pretend I don't need a challenging job.

▨ When someone asks me to do something I prefer not to do, I do it reluctantly and won't put my heart into it.

▨ I use indifference to cover up my low opinion of myself.

We use rebellion and defiance as a way to disguise the ADD traits that make us feel "different" from others.

▨ People call me a maverick, and accuse me of being a nonconformist.

I act like a tough guy to hide my feelings of inferiority and to make others think I am more important than I feel.

I dress and behave in ways that defy the norm, and am criticized for my weird ways.

As a teenager, I loved to cause trouble and keep my teachers and parents upset.

We are defensive and respond poorly to personal criticism or teasing.

When others criticize me, I become defensive and take it as meaning that something is wrong with me because I have ADD.

I like to tease others, but when others tease me, it hurts my feelings.

I avoid people who are sarcastic or who have been hurtful to me in the past.

When someone questions a decision I make, I become defensive and try hard to justify my reason for the decision.

We have difficulty in sexual relationships; we use sex as a source of high stimulation, or we consider sex uninteresting or a bothersome distraction.

I use sex as a way to keep excitement in my life.

When I want sex, I can be very demanding and intolerant of my partner's needs.

I am told I am frigid, because I appear uninterested when engaging in sexual activity.

I have difficulty becoming aroused because my mind drifts somewhere else.

We have a compelling need for excitement and high stimulation in our lives.

I look for excitement and high stimulation to distract me and keep me interested.

I love action movies.

I engage in high-risk activities like car racing, motorcycling, scuba diving, roller-blading.

I love the idea of going to Las Vegas for a weekend or spending a day at the races with my partner, where I can gamble and feel the excitement that gambling brings.

We use co-dependent and caretaking behavior to feel better about ourselves and avoid abandonment or rejection.

▪ I feel threatened when others disapprove of me, and am terrified of rejection.

▪ I become enmeshed in other peoples' lives and want to be involved in everything they do.

▪ I deny my own feelings and focus my attention on meeting the needs of others.

▪ When I am busy taking care of others, it takes the focus off me, and I don't have to face my own issues.

We use denial as a survival tool to protect ourselves from reality.

▪ I protect myself from reality by pretending that things are different than they really are.

▪ I minimize the powerful impact that ADD has on my life, rather than face it and take steps to correct it.

▪ I find excuses for my behavior because that is easier than dealing with it.

▪ I use anger as a way to deny what is really happening. It keeps me from identifying my true feelings and gives me an excuse for not addressing the core issue.

We use manipulation and control to manage our lives and make our ADD symptoms more tolerable.

▪ I deal with the confusion of my life by trying to manipulate people and things.

▪ I attempt to control others through pity, guilt, charm, humor, and sex.

▪ I sometimes use physical or verbal force to control others.

▪ I make up stories about myself to give people the impression that I am in control.

We tend to isolate ourselves and feel uncomfortable around other people.

▪ Keeping my distance from others protects me from ridicule, shame, and embarrassment.

▪ When I have a craving for absolute quiet, I go to the park or get in my car and drive around with no destination in mind.

▪ I prefer not to be noticed at parties. Sometimes I don't even say hello or goodbye, and this offends people.

▪ I feel uncomfortable when others draw attention to me. It reminds me of my school days, when my teachers humiliated me in front of my classmates.

We have a strong desire to escape from the ADD symptoms that negatively affect us.

▪ I daydream about early retirement, so I can stop all the craziness and learn to relax.

▪ I use addictive behavior to escape from the pain and discomfort of living with ADD.

▪ I will quit a job or end a relationship so that I don't have to conform to accepted standards of behaving and relating.

▪ I look forward to vacations, hoping that I will find some peace and serenity and be free from the chaos in my life.

Positive Qualities
Find the good. It's all around you.
Find it, showcase it, and you'll start believing in it.
And so will most of the people who come into
contact with you.
—JESSE OWENS

This exercise will help you identify with the qualities that many adults with ADD possess. You will not identify with every one. But for those with which you do, make note of how they apply to you.

We are intelligent, and highly motivated by intellectual challenges.
- As a child, I was praised for my abilities.
- I can grasp the meaning of a business presentation before the speaker finishes talking.
- I often have answers to questions before others do, and I am sometimes called a whiz kid.
- Although I used to daydream in class and not pay attention to the teacher, I still got good grades.

We are creative and highly imaginative, and can express ourselves in unique ways.
- I am an idea person and can solve problems quickly. In the midst of craziness, I often show signs of creative brilliance.
- I express myself in creative ways through music, drama, writing, or art.
- I have a talent for expressing my feelings on paper.
- I roam from one idea to the next. This often brings surprising opportunities.

We have high energy and meet challenges with enthusiasm.
- Others tell me they get tired just watching me or feeling my energy vibes.
- I am most productive when a lot of energy is required to complete a task.

▦ Thanks to my high energy level, I am equipped to meet the demands I place on myself.

▦ I am competitive, and have a take-charge attitude about life.

We are intuitive and can easily sense the needs and feelings of others.

▦ I have a sixth sense and often know that something is going to happen before it actually does. Some people call me psychic.

▦ I can sense when my children are hurting, or when they have something to say but can't express themselves.

▦ I sense others' feelings without their telling me how they feel. I can read body language.

▦ My intuition and ability to hyperfocus helps me to recognize that a problem exists before it is identified or presented.

We are resourceful, and can devise ways and means to accomplish things.

▦ In the midst of uncertainty, I look for ways to find stability, and can usually find them.

▦ I take advantage of opportunities and am always looking for new ways to do things.

▦ I can find answers to problems that baffle others.

▦ When an opportunity is lost, I usually find another one to take its place.

We are warmhearted and enjoy doing things for others.

▦ I can sense when others are hurting, and take time to offer comfort and support.

▦ I feel a sense of achievement when I do something for others, and don't expect anything in return.

▦ People are drawn to me because of my warmhearted nature.

▦ I feel sad when someone close to me is sad, and I try to help wherever possible.

We are humorous and have an ability to make others laugh.

▦ I enjoy being the life of the party.

▦ In school, I was considered the class clown.

■ When there is an awkward moment in a conversation or social gathering, I find it easy to break the ice by saying or doing something funny.

■ I can see humor in a serious situation when others are looking only at the downside.

We are hardworking, and have a never-say-die approach to life.

■ When I like my work, I give it everything I've got.

■ I enjoy working hard if it has a potential for bringing positive results.

■ I will put in extra hours at work, then come home and start another project.

■ People are often amazed by my productivity.

We are willing to take risks, and see risk-taking as a form of excitement.

■ If I believe strongly in something, I will pursue it regardless of the risk involved.

■ I take risks and do not worry about the downside potential. My philosophy is "No guts, no glory."

■ I like to go against the odds and risk failure, believing that success is highly possible.

■ I take risks by expressing myself honestly.

We are loyal, honest, and trustworthy.

■ I am loyal to my friends, family, and co-workers.

■ When I make a commitment, I keep it.

■ I am honest with others, and I say what I think. Even though I sometimes make an inappropriate comment, people don't have to wonder what I am thinking.

■ I do not easily let go of someone or something I care about.

We are flexible, and adapt easily to change.

■ When a sudden change occurs, I look forward to the challenge that change brings.

■ When obstacles get in my way, I find other things to do, rather than become angry.

■ I can roll with the punches and go with the flow.

▨ My ability to be flexible is a gift that helps me deal with my friends, spouse, and children. When they don't bend, I do.

We are change agents, and like the intrigue involved in change.
▨ If I see a need for taking a different approach to something, I can make change happen by stirring the pot.
▨ I tend to criticize the status quo and resist authority.
▨ When I am in a situation where things are losing ground, I quickly look for alternative methods to improve the conditions.
▨ I keep changing gears at home so my family has intrigue and variety, and so I don't become impatient or frustrated from lack of excitement.

We are good observers and are able to find quick solutions to complicated situations.
▨ I observe things, people, and events that others may not notice.
▨ When my children are having difficulties, I like to help them find an easy solution.
▨ I am interested in life and world events.
▨ I see beyond minor details, and can sort out what is important.

We are productive and effective if we like what we are doing.
▨ If I know the bottom line and like what I am doing, I can get a lot done.
▨ I am motivated when others praise me and offer me support and encouragement.
▨ I can focus on multiple tasks at the same time.
▨ I produce quick results when it is important to do so.

We are forgiving, and rarely hold grudges.
▨ I am able to move past petty differences and see what is really important.
▨ I forgive easily and don't hold a grudge for an extended period of time.
▨ I make mistakes on a regular basis, so I don't criticize others when they make them.
▨ I don't always forget the wrongs that are done, but I am willing to forgive if the person is truly sorry.

REVIEW OF RESENTMENTS

	COLUMN 1	COLUMN 2
	I resent	**because**
	My boss	*he doesn't listen to me*
1		
2		
3		
4		
5		
6		
7		
8		
9		
10		

INSTRUCTIONS FOR COMPLETION

Column 1 List the people, institutions, or principles you resent, including the childhood resentments that still affect you. Complete column 1 from top to bottom before going to column 2.

Column 2 List what happened to cause the resentment. Complete column 2 from top to bottom before going to column 3.

COLUMN 3	COLUMN 4
This affects my	**The nature of my wrongs were**
self-esteem	*anger and defiance*

Column 3 List your needs or ambitions that were affected. Needs include social needs (self-esteem, relationship); security needs (material, emotional); sexual needs. Ambitions include social, security, and sexual ambitions. Complete column 3 before going to column 4.

Column 4 List the nature of your wrongs, faults, mistakes, defects, or shortcomings that surfaced because of the resentment. These include anger, co-dependency, defiance, dishonesty, disrespect, envy, impatience, impulsivity, irresponsibility, lust, manipulation, selfishness.

Finally Read from left to right and see who you resented, why you are resentful, which of your needs were threatened, and the exact nature of the wrong that caused your resentment and blocked you from God's will.

REVIEW OF FEARS

	COLUMN 1	COLUMN 2
	I fear	**because**
	My spouse	*I can never please her*
1		
2		
3		
4		
5		
6		
7		
8		
9		
10		

INSTRUCTIONS FOR COMPLETION

Column 1 List the people, institutions, or principles you fear, including the childhood fears that still affect you. Complete column 1 from top to bottom before going to column 2.

Column 2 List what happened to cause the fear. Complete column 2 from top to bottom before going to column 3.

COLUMN 3	COLUMN 4
This affects my	**The nature of my wrongs were**
emotional and sexual needs	*co-dependency and anger*

Column 3 List your needs or ambitions that were affected. Needs include social needs (self-esteem, relationship); security needs (material, emotional); sexual needs. Ambitions include social, security, and sexual ambitions. Complete column 3 before going to column 4.

Column 4 List the nature of your wrongs, faults, mistakes, defects, or shortcomings that surfaced because of the fear. These include anger, co-dependency, defiance, dishonesty, disrespect, envy, impatience, impulsivity, irresponsibility, lust, manipulation, selfishness.

Finally Read from left to right and see who you feared, why you are fearful, which of your needs were threatened, and the exact nature of the wrong that caused your fear and blocked you from God's will.

REVIEW OF HARMFUL CONDUCT

	COLUMN 1	COLUMN 2
	I harmed	**by**
	My son	*embarrassing and punishing him*
1		
2		
3		
4		
5		
6		
7		
8		
9		
10		

INSTRUCTIONS FOR COMPLETION

Column 1 List the people who were affected by your harmful conduct. Complete column 1 from top to bottom before going to column 2.

Column 2 List what happened to cause the harmful conduct. Complete column 2 from top to bottom before going to column 3.

108

COLUMN 3	COLUMN 4
This affects my	**The nature of my wrongs were**
relationship with him and sets a bad example	*disrespect and manipulation*

Column 3 List your needs or ambitions that were affected. Needs include social needs (self-esteem, relationship); security needs (material, emotional); sexual needs. Ambitions include social, security, and sexual ambitions. Complete column 3 before going to column 4.

Column 4 List the nature of your wrongs, faults, mistakes, defects, or shortcomings that surfaced because of the harmful conduct. These include anger, co-dependency, defiance, dishonesty, disrespect, envy, impatience, impulsivity, irresponsibility, lust, manipulation, selfishness.

Finally Read from left to right and see who you harmed, why you harmed them, which of your needs were threatened, and the exact nature of the wrong that caused your harmful behavior and blocked you from God's will.

I was afraid that my inventory would cause me a lot of pain, but it was easier than I thought it would be. The most important things I learned about myself are:

_____

_____

_____

_____

_____

_____

_____

_____

_____

_____

_____

_____

_____

_____

_____

_____

_____

_____

STEP FOUR REVIEW

Step Four is a tool to help us understand our current behavior patterns and recognize our need for God's guidance in our lives. Here we examine our behavior and expand our understanding of ourselves. Being thorough and honest in preparing our inventory helps us see the obstacles that have prevented us from knowing ourselves and acknowledging our deepest feelings about life.

❑ What is your most positive quality, and how does it support you?

❑ Which of your behaviors are most damaging to your life? Explain.

❑ In what ways do tend to hide from reality?

❑ What negative messages about yourself plague you and cause you to fear this inventory process?

5

UNDERSTANDING STEP FIVE

Imagine a stuffy and odor-filled house that's been shut up for years. We can't wait to open the doors, pull back the drapes, and ventilate the rooms. Our lives are like closed-up houses. All our shameful secrets, selfish attitudes, embarrassing behaviors, and spoiled hopes lie hidden from view. The atmosphere of our lives is stale because we have kept the doors and windows closed to anyone else lest we be found out, rejected, or shamed. Step Five is our coming-out celebration—we open the doors and windows. Freshness floods in as we finally see our real selves.

WORKING STEP FIVE

Step Five is a continuation of Step Four, where we share the nature of our wrongs with God. Then we take an honest and objective look at ourselves and reflect on our discoveries. Lastly, we share our inventory with someone who will understand and encourage us. In the past, we found many ways to isolate ourselves, but now that we are gaining a better perspective, and we want to change and grow. Like someone going out on an important date, we ask, "How do I look? How can I improve? What do you see that I don't?"

PREPARING FOR STEP FIVE

We prepare for Step Five by asking God for the willingness to accept an outsider's opinion and feedback. The person with whom we share our inventory will be more objective than we are and will see motivations, behavior patterns, and character flaws that escape our view. We need the help of our Higher Power to receive the feedback if we are to see the "exact nature of our wrongs."

STEP FIVE

Admitted to God, to ourselves, and to another human being the exact nature of our wrongs.

Once we have taken this step, withholding nothing, we are delighted. We can look the world in the eye. We can be alone at perfect peace and ease. Our fears fall from us. We begin to feel the nearness of our Creator. We may have had certain spiritual beliefs, but now we begin to have a spiritual experience. —ALCOHOLICS ANONYMOUS (THIRD EDITION, PAGE 75)

The first four Steps made us aware of many truths about ourselves and laid the foundation for Step Five. In Step One, we understood the problem and looked at its true nature. In Step Two, we accepted the existence of a Power greater than ourselves. In Step Three, we decided to turn our lives over to that Power. In Step Four we began searching for the root of our problems. We were able to see the difference between the ADD behavior we can't control and the character traits and behavior we can change with God's help. We now have a better understanding of how we coped with our condition and protected ourselves against the abusive treatment and disapproval of others.

> *Step Five requires fact-facing, willingness to expose yourself to others. Try to be aware of how you are feeling, and don't become Hungry, Angry, Lonely, or Tired. A program saying is HALT. It can work wonders if you repeat it when you feel yourself slipping.*

Facing our self-defeating behavior, shortcomings, and wrongs can cause a lot of pain and discomfort. The natural reaction is to feel sadness or guilt, or both. In Step Four, we faced ourselves honestly and identified behaviors that we want and need to eliminate. If our inventory was honest and thorough, Step Four provided the foundation of self-understanding we need to ensure lasting recovery. In Step Five we will improve upon our inventory and self-understanding by sharing our faults with others. With the help of God, ourselves, and another human being, we will examine and expose the "exact nature of our wrongs."

Parts of me are really scared to share my life story with someone else. I'm going to take a risk and ask my therapist to hear my fifth Step. He's an outsider I can trust and isn't emotionally involved. Even though my therapist is not a friend, I feel that I can be sincere, and he will help me to speak my thoughts honestly and openly.

Christie's Story

Dear Paul,

I'm writing you because it's impossible to talk to you in person. You're so busy and important that I rarely see you. When you are home, you won't sit still long enough to talk, and if you do sit down, you only pretend to be listening. You're too unpredictable and moody, and explode over the strangest things and at the weirdest times. I don't think you know how to relax and enjoy life. You expect me to be physically intimate with you, yet you can't be emotionally intimate with me. It seems like every conversation we have is some kind of a challenge to you, rather than a means of sharing our thoughts and feelings. A simple conversation often turns into an argument—or a problem you try to solve. Your energy level exhausts me, your demands intimidate me, and your needs overwhelm me.

I don't like myself anymore. I've become an expert at sulking and deception, and I've even talked myself into believing I could change you. Now I'm frightened, Paul, because I don't think I love you anymore. All I think about is finding someone who will care about me, take time for me, and make me feel special. I know it sounds selfish, but it's what is going on inside my head. The only reason I'm still here is because of Pauly. But the older he gets, the more he's like you. That doesn't feel good either, and it makes me even more miserable.

Please don't misunderstand me. I know you think you've made progress. I agree that the medicine and counseling have helped your ADD, but you aren't any different. You still act like you're the only one in the world who matters. You lord it over me, you're harsh with Pauly, and you never accept or admit any blame. Everything is always my fault.

A part of me wants to believe there's hope for us, but I'm really not sure any more. If there is, it's up to you to find it. I'm tired of being the only one who tries, and I'm sure I'll learn to adjust if we're apart.

Your wife,
Christie

The behavior characteristics associated with ADD can put a great deal of stress on intimate relationships. Work together as a team and set some guidelines for improving communication and resolving the power struggles between you. Some helpful hints: schedule time for talking, declare a truce if necessary, and make lists of things that need to be done.

Our growing relationship with God gives us the courage to examine ourselves, accept who we are, and reveal our true nature. Step Five helps us acknowledge and discard our old survival skills and move toward a new and healthier life. We do this by admitting our wrongs and gaining a better understanding of what we did and why we did it. Being thorough and honest in completing our inventory places us in a position to face the facts clearly and move forward.

Step Five requires that we engage in some honest self-confrontation by admitting our faults to God, to ourselves, and to another person. By doing so, we get an outside opinion and a different look at things. We gain a better perspective of how others perceive us; in turn, we learn more about our behavior. For some of us, this will involve telling our life story for the first time. As we tell our story, we begin to cleanse ourselves of the excess baggage we have been carrying around for most of our lives. As we open our hearts and reveal ourselves, we will achieve a deeper level of spirituality.

I decided to put down my guard and look honestly at myself. It's helped me to see that a lot of my wrongs are because of ADD—not because I am a bad person. Now that I'm in a twelve-step program, I know I can overcome a lot of the difficulties I have with myself and others.

Admitting the exact nature of our wrongs to God is the first phase of Step Five. Here we share with God what we uncovered about ourselves in Step Four. We know now there's no reason to blame God or others for what happened to us. We see how self-will blocked us from God's will and how we used denial as a shield against seeing the true impact of ADD and its effect on our well-being. In Step Five we begin to accept our ADD and its resulting behavior for exactly what they are. We admit the "exact nature of our wrongs" and assume responsibility for our actions. We must remember that we are children of a loving God and will never be rejected. Our Higher Power will strengthen and guide us as we seek to lead a healthier and more peaceful life.

> *Studies show that adults with ADD spend as much as 80 percent of their day with distractions, and only 20 percent doing what they need to do. Give yourself permission to eliminate potential distractions when you are preparing for Step Five. The more time you can devote to it, the more chance you have for success. Distractions can be greatly lessened by turning off the phone, going to a quiet place, or simply closing the door. Others may accuse you of isolating yourself, or being antisocial, but for someone with ADD, such actions are common sense.*

Admitting our wrongs to ourselves began in Step Four, as we wrote our inventory and had the opportunity to see our behavior for what it really is. In Step Five we consciously admit our wrongs to ourselves and gain a new perspective on our lives. Our admission to ourselves is the least-threatening part of Step Five, and can be done with the least risk. But it is not the easiest part of Step Five because of our tendency to deny reality. We use denial as a coping mechanism—an unconscious tool to protect ourselves from pain. Denial protects us from facing the truth about ourselves. It is not easily conquered, but if we have done an honest Step Four inventory, the barrier of denial is already weakened.

Telling our story to another person can be a frightening experience, especially if we're conditioned to constant ridicule and judgment from others. It puts a crack in our armor when we have to expose ourselves to someone and be totally honest. Many of us exert a lot of energy building defenses protect ourselves and to keep others out. In order to "pass for normal," we limit our contact with others as much as possible. Step Five is our pathway out of isolation and loneliness and a move toward wholeness, happiness, and peace.

In the process of admitting the "exact nature of our wrongs" to another person, we will discover parts of ourselves that were hidden from view. Sharing with another person will help us expand our moral inventory and see motivations, patterns, and blind spots that were hidden before. By exposing ourselves verbally we will recognize some self-defeating behaviors and character traits that we relied upon to maintain a sense of sanity and stability in our lives. If we encourage feedback and accept it as positive criticism, we will come to know a new freedom and be less resentful and fearful.

For our admission to another human being, we need to select an understanding person who is not involved, and who can look at our inventory as an outsider. The person must be dependable, objective, and willing to confront us if necessary. It is wise to choose someone who is familiar with ADD and the Twelve Steps. Trusting the person with whom we share our story is vital to the success of Step Five and will provide a safe atmosphere for full disclosure and feedback.

In telling our story to another person, we need more than a sounding board. We must be willing to listen to the other person's response and accept his or her opinions. This openness is vital as a means of completing the process of self-understanding and identifying clearly what we must eliminate from our behavior. We should be clear about what kind of feedback we want, and before we begin we should establish an understanding with the other person. The more receptive we are to feedback, the better our chances for achieving the personality change that can happen when we successfully complete Step Five.

Procrastination may interfere with your ability to complete Step Five. Take time to develop a plan and set a schedule for doing your fifth Step. Remember, if you have trouble getting started, start anyway! Even if your plan seems overly simple, just start it. The rest will come easily.

After completing Step Five, we may wonder what to do with our new knowledge. In a sense, Step Five is like looking in a mirror and finding that we have dirt on our face. To walk away would mean that we return to denial and ignore the dirt. To stay and try to clean it off by ourselves would be to return to our self-will. The truth is that we cannot remove the dirt without help. It is an indelible mark put there by our own hand. God doesn't expect us to be able to change ourselves, and God doesn't want us to return to denial. God wants us to embrace our new awareness of our wrongs and be willing to let the necessary changes occur.

For many adults with ADD, depression is a way of life. It can coexist with ADD and cause a lot of unpredictable mood swings. Often it can be attributed to a sense of frustration and failure, a sense of loss, or a result of living with an overflow of energy and an under-supply of self-esteem. Learn all you can about ADD and how to manage your moods. Proper rest, a healthy diet, and regular exercise can relieve some forms of depression. Changing the scenery and having a structured "blow-out" time also helps. When the scenery changes, the mood often changes too, regardless of what's going on in the external world.

Seeing ourselves in a new light doesn't mean we are ready and willing to have God change us immediately. A drastic change means throwing away our crutches and getting rid of behaviors that have been our survival skills, our painkillers, and our means of coping with ADD and life itself. To think of letting go and having to stand on our own two feet can be like letting go of old, reliable friends. The fear of loss can cause us to feel depressed or anxious. Even though we know these friends are a bad influence on us, the idea of saying goodbye to them is scary.

Key Ideas

Wrongs: The wrongs that we admit in Step Five are the behaviors, traits, and shortcomings that surface when our self-will compels us to act on our resentments and fears. Admitting these wrongs prepares us for Step Seven, where we ask to have them removed.

Resentments and fears: Recognizing our resentments and fears and our reaction to them provides helpful clues to understanding ourselves and our behavior. Like clues to a buried treasure, our resentments and fears point us toward a deeper understanding of what is in our hearts. Once we identify the objects of our resentments and fears, we find clues that uncover their causes and the parts of ourselves that were threatened. Our reaction to the threat provides our final clue. It discloses the damaging behaviors, survival skills, and character traits that result from self-will and self-reliance. This process of following the clues can become a life-long method of coping with our behavior.

"The exact nature": In column four of our inventory worksheet we noted the "exact nature" of our resentments, fears, or harmful conduct. We identified the faults that surfaced when we felt threatened. These defects—addiction, anger, compulsion, control, dishonesty, disrespect, envy, lust, pride, and selfishness—arise when we rely on self-will rather than on God's will. When we understand the "exact nature of our wrongs," we can take responsibility for them and begin the process of getting rid of them.

Prayer for Step Five

Higher Power,
My inventory has shown me who I am,
Yet I ask for your help in admitting my wrongs
To another person and to you.
Assure me, and be with me in this Step,
For without this Step I cannot progress in my recovery.
With your help, I can do this, and I will do it.

STEP FIVE EXERCISE

Admitting the Exact Nature of Your Wrongs
A fault confessed is a new virtue added to a man.
—JAMES S. KNOWLES

Guidelines for Completing Step Five

- Step Five involves admitting the exact nature of your wrongs to God, to yourself, and to another human being. You admit how your traits, behaviors, attitudes, and faults were hurtful to yourself and to others. It is not necessary to discuss how the wrongs came about or how you plan to make the necessary changes. You are not seeking counsel or advice.

- The objective is to improve upon your inventory by looking at your positive qualities as well as your character defects. Step Five can bring those qualities into sharper focus with help from an understanding listener.

- Begin with prayer by calling upon your Higher Power to be present as you prepare to review the inventory you made in Step Four. Ask God to guide and support you in what you are about to experience.

- After completing Step Five, take time to pray, meditate, and reflect on what you accomplished. Thank your Higher Power for the gifts you are receiving as a result of your growing spirituality. Spend time rereading the first five Steps and note anything you omitted. The cornerstone is your relationship with God and your commitment to honesty and humility.

- Congratulate yourself for having the courage to risk self-disclosure, and thank God for the peace of mind that this program brings.

Guidelines for Completing Step Five with God

▣ Avoid the tendency to procrastinate. Make an appointment with yourself now to complete Step Five with God.

Date _____ Time _____ Place _____

▣ Step Five is for your own benefit—God already knows you. You are beginning a process of living a life of humility, honesty, and courage. The result is freedom, happiness, and serenity.

▣ Think of an image that gives you the feeling of a physical connection with God. A way to do this is to put a chair in front of you for God. Or go to a church sanctuary and imagine God at the altar. You can also meet God in the majesty of nature or through the eyes of a beloved pet. Choose a way that works for you and gives you a sense of meeting with God.

▣ Your ADD traits affect your focus and cause you to be restless, distracted, impulsive, or forgetful at times. So plan now to take regular breaks and reduce the tendency to become bored and lose interest. Use a doodle pad to jot down all the ideas and urges you will undoubtedly have. Plan to be yourself—fidget and wiggle or pull at your hair if necessary.

▣ Start with a prayer such as, "God, I understand that you already know me, and you won't judge me for my inattentiveness. I am now ready to reveal all of myself to you openly and humbly. I am grateful to you for the gifts and abilities you gave me to get me to this point in my life. Take away my fear of ridicule and rejection as I place myself in your care and keeping."

▣ Imagine that your Higher Power is visibly with you, and speak audibly, sincerely, and honestly. Share your understanding of the insights you gained from your inventory in Step Four. Be aware that emotions may surface as part of the powerful cleansing experience taking place.

Guidelines for Completing Step Five with Yourself

▦ Avoid the tendency to procrastinate. Make an appointment with yourself right now to complete Step Five with yourself.

Date _____ Time _____ Place _____

▦ In Step Four you began the process of self-discovery and genuine self-love. Solitary self-appraisal begins your admission to yourself, but it alone is not enough. In Step Five you improve upon your own self-knowledge and move toward self-acceptance. Like many people with ADD, you may have trouble accepting what you discover about yourself. In your attempts to "pass for normal," you may have lost your own identity. Step Five helps you reestablish your identity and gain a new measure of self-acceptance.

▦ Sit in a chair with your imaginary double seated across from you, or sit in front of a mirror.

▦ Your ADD traits may cause you to get restless, be distracted, have impulses to do other things, or forget what you're supposed to be doing. So plan now to take regular breaks and reduce the tendency to become bored and lose interest. Use a doodle pad to jot down all the ideas and urges you will undoubtedly have. Plan to be yourself—fidget and wiggle or pull at your hair if necessary.

▦ Share your moral inventory with yourself, including your character defects and positive qualities.

▦ Speak out loud and allow yourself time to hear what you are saying. Take notes on any deeper understanding that surfaces.

▦ Acknowledge your courage for reaching this point. Every part of this process releases excess emotional baggage that you carried around because of your lifelong struggle to compensate for ADD and its related behavior.

Guidelines for Choosing Someone with Whom to Share Step Five

- Ask for God's help in choosing the person to whom you will admit your wrongs—someone who is not emotionally involved and can be objective. This person should be familiar with ADD and the Twelve Steps.

- Look for someone with qualities that you admire and that will inspire your confidence. The person should be on an equal spiritual level with a similar understanding of God. Sharing your personal experiences with another person will help you come to know the depth of God's unconditional love for all humanity.

- Choose a listener who is patient and sympathetic. The listener is God's spokesperson and will communicate God's unconditional acceptance.

- Choose your listener carefully. The listener can be 1) an ordained priest or minister; 2) a trusted friend, doctor, or psychologist; or 3) a family member with whom you can openly share, and who is not emotionally involved.

Guidelines for Completing Step Five with Another Person

- Avoid the tendency to procrastinate. Make an appointment with yourself now to complete Step Five with another person.

  Date _____ Time _____ Place _____

- Considerable humility and courage are needed to bare our souls to another person. It is a bold step toward eliminating our need to be like others—to "pass for normal."

- Tell your listener your preference for feedback. Questions to ask yourself are: 1) Do I want to be interrupted if the listener has a question or has something to offer? 2) Can I handle constructive criticism? 3) Do I want prayer and praise as part of the input?

▪ Eliminate distractions such as telephone calls, children, visitors, and extraneous noises. To avoid getting frustrated and bored, you may need to conduct the meeting in a place that can include another activity such as a walk or scenic ride. Take breaks if necessary and do what works for you.

▪ Speak clearly, sincerely, and honestly and share your understanding of insights gained from your moral inventory. Be aware that emotions may surface as part of the powerful cleansing experience taking place, and allow time to process these feelings. They are a key factor in successfully completing Step Five.

▪ Allow ample time to complete each thought, and stay focused on the subject. Refrain from unnecessary explanations and follow written notes.

▪ Allow plenty of time for feedback from the other person. When you finish Step Five, share your feelings about the experience with each other.

STEP FIVE REVIEW

Step Five requires that we engage in honest confrontations with ourselves and others by admitting our faults to God, to ourselves, and to another person. By doing so, we begin to set aside our pride and see ourselves in true perspective. We also realize how our growing relationship with our Higher Power gives us the courage to examine ourselves, accept who we are, and reveal our true selves. Step Five helps us acknowledge and become ready to discard our old survival skills and move toward a new and healthier life.

❑ What can be gained by admitting your faults to another person?

❑ What form of denial do people say you use to avoid reality or responsibility (blaming, rationalizing, minimizing, etc.)? Explain.

❑ Which of your faults is the most difficult to acknowledge to another? Why?

❑ In what ways will admitting your wrongs to God, to yourself, and to another person help you to stop deceiving yourself?

6

UNDERSTANDING STEP SIX

When a farmer plants a crop, he begins by preparing the soil. He will plow, disc, harrow, fertilize, and plant. Then he stops and allows the seeds to grow. In Step Six, activity ceases for a season. We allow the seeds of change that God planted to germinate. We give our emotions a chance to catch up with our new experiences. We have plowed and prepared. Now we give God time to create an internal change—a willingness to let go of what we know is wrong.

WORKING STEP SIX

From now on, the process is about change. To lose weight we have to stop eating some foods we really like: candy, fast food, etc. Even though we like those foods, we don't like what we see in the mirror. So we deny ourselves and eat some foods we don't like: salads, vegetables, and low-calorie items. When we do this, we will see some positive changes in our bodies. Other people will see the changes too, and we may begin to prefer the new foods. The same changes are occurring in our personalities. We start replacing our resentments, fears, and anger with love, tolerance, and patience. We feel better about ourselves, have fewer problems, and develop healthier relationships.

PREPARING FOR STEP SIX

We prepare for Step Six by quieting our minds and opening our hearts to God's plan for us. Steps Four and Five required a lot of soul-searching and brought up some painful discoveries about ourselves. Now we prepare for the next leg of the journey by making quiet time for ourselves. We take time to be alone with ourselves and with God by removing the distractions that can shield us from reality.

STEP SIX

Were entirely ready to have God remove all these defects of character.

If it's peace you want, seek change for yourself, not other people. It is easier to protect your feet with slippers than to carpet the whole world.

—ANONYMOUS

Step Six is a step of the heart. We become ready to say goodbye to old friends—habits we now see in a new light. Although this means letting go of wrong attitudes, self-defeating behavior, flawed character traits, and other faults, we sometimes balk at the idea. We hesitate because these character traits and behaviors have been our survival skills, our painkillers, and our means of coping with ADD. To actually let go feels like letting go of trusted allies on whom we have come to depend. We know these friends have been bad influences, but saying goodbye is bitter medicine, and may cause us to wonder if we will be lonely and bored.

Candy's Story

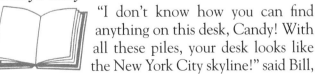 "I don't know how you can find anything on this desk, Candy! With all these piles, your desk looks like the New York City skyline!" said Bill, the science department head. He mumbled something else as he shook his head and laughed, but Candy didn't see the humor. She pretended to be in

control for Bill's sake, but the truth was, she couldn't make any sense of the papers on her desk. With the semester nearing an end, she needed to sort through and find everything, then grade the papers, tests, and book reports.

After Bill left, all Candy could do was stand and stare at her desk and wonder what to do next. Her mind froze while her heart raced. She felt as though a demon had entered her chest and grabbed her throat. All she could think about was going home, but two periods remained. In the meantime, the papers on her desk sat there as a reminder of all the things she hated about herself. What hurt most was having to look straight at her sloth, disorganization, procrastination, and mismanagement.

When Candy finally got home, she walked past the answering machine without listening to messages, took the phone off the hook, added the day's mail to the stack, then opened the refrigerator to look for her friend—the one who would make everything okay. The cork squeaked. The glass chimed as the bottle kissed its rim. Finally Candy could stop, relax, and center herself for a brief moment. The papers would be easier to grade after she'd relaxed. But before Candy realized it, the bottle was empty and the night was gone. The papers and tests would have to wait for yet another night, when she felt better and could think clearly.

I'm really proud of the new person who is developing inside me. But some of my family members, friends, and co-workers are still angry and resentful, and they don't believe I can change. What they don't know is how good I feel inside. I'm willing to be patient and stay focused on "me." Someday I'm sure they'll notice the change. Who knows? They might even throw an affirming word my way!

We've spent our whole life developing the behaviors and traits that we now know are harmful. In Step Six we begin the actual process of change. The first five Steps prepared us for change by making us aware of our objectionable behavior. In Step One, we saw the problem and admitted it. In Step Two, we saw the solution by "coming to believe," then made a decision in Step Three to turn our lives over to God's care. Step Four gave us the tools to identify our resentments, fears, and problem behavior. Admitting the "exact nature of our wrongs" in Step Five paved the way for letting go of the traits and behavior we no longer need. God knows our uniqueness, and realizes that some of our problems result from ADD. By putting our trust in our Higher Power, we will discover what we can and can't change.

Our character defects, the things that must change in our lives, are called many things in twelve-step programs—weaknesses, faults, shortcomings, harmful behaviors, survival skills, negative traits, etc. Whatever the name, the message is the same. These undesirable parts of ourselves that have caused us so much trouble must be removed and replaced with desirable ones. These character defects began innocently in childhood as survival techniques to cope with our environment. We manipulated to have our needs met, lied to protect ourselves, and buried our emotions in defense against pain. We did these things to manage our environment, minimize our threats, and take care of ourselves. Eventually these coping skills stop working. When they do, we realize that God is the only one able and wise enough to control our lives.

We are not expected to remove our character defects alone. All we're asked to do is become ready and willing to "let

If scattered papers are a problem for you, use colored folders and tabs to create attractive files. Discipline yourself to throw papers away if they serve no purpose. Save only the ones you need, but find a home for them.

go and let God." Step Six does not require action from us. It represents a state of preparation that readies us to release our faults to God. Our willingness to surrender will increase as we recognize how much happier we can be once we actually change our behavior. This willingness enables us to reach the point in Step Seven where we ask God to take over and remove our shortcomings. We accomplish this by working the program one day at a time, regardless of whether or not we see any progress.

> *Studies show that adults with ADD often say that fear is one of the most troubling and life-controlling emotions they feel. Common fears include fear of others, fear of failure, and fear of learning new things. Once fear is overcome, it is replaced with courage.*

The idea of changing our behavior can cause fear and anxiety. We tend to cling to what we are because it is familiar—not because we like what we are. One part of us wants to throw out what we don't like, but another part resists making changes because of the uncertainty of the outcome. When we can effectively deal with this fear and anxiety, the process of change starts to happen. We learn that, as we get rid of negative traits, positive ones appear and take their place. We replace hate with love, fear with courage, impatience with tolerance, and find fewer and fewer problems with people. We begin to feel secure in the knowledge of God's love and perfect plan for our lives.

Step Six offers a time to overcome fear and gather the readiness we need to proceed with our recovery. In Step Six we develop readiness and willingness to allow God to change us. This step is like bungee jumping. You may be dressed to jump and have all the facts about the bungee cord, but you won't jump until you're ready. And you won't be ready until you overcome your fear.

Your defects are a part of you; they have helped you survive. The thought of losing anything, even your damaging defects, makes you afraid.

Step Six is similar to Step Two. Both Steps deal with our willingness to allow God to work through us to change our lives. In Step Two we sought restoration to sanity by coming to believe in a Power greater than ourselves. In Step Six we seek readiness to let God remove our shortcomings. Both Steps acknowledge the existence of problems and require that we seek God's help and guidance to free us from them. The fact that we "came to believe" will strengthen our capacity to be "entirely ready."

Prayer is an important part of Step Six. But we need to talk with God in a way that shows our humility and our need for God's intervention. When we say, "Dear God, make me more patient," we are telling God what to do. That sort of prayer tends to reinforce our self-will. On the other hand, when we say "Dear God, I am impatient,"

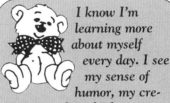

I know I'm learning more about myself every day. I see my sense of humor, my creativity, and my high energy level. I have some negative traits because of ADD, but I know that when I'm ready, I'll ask God to remove them.

we present the truth about ourselves, and leave "what to do" in God's hands. When we pray in this manner, we exhibit humility, relinquish our pride, and ask God to act on our behalf.

This Step requires that we look at our shortcomings so we can ask God to remove them. We may be unwilling to give up some of them because they may seem useful to us. We need to be honest with God and say, "God, I'm still afraid to give up _____ . Please help me to overcome my fear, so I can be entirely ready to ask you to remove it from me. "What is important is that we become willing to let go of our shortcomings and trust that their removal will bring us positive results. When we do this it will open the door to a new way of

> Step Six involves a willingness to change. This is an excellent time to reevaluate your medications. Medicine is a wonderful tool when properly used, but it isn't the total answer. As you work the Steps and learn more about your spiritual side, your need for certain medication may diminish. Talk to your doctor, and be honest with him or her.

living, and our old traits will be replaced by new ones that are better for us.

We must guard against the negative tapes and self-talk that might make us believe we will never be any different. The fact that we have attention deficit disorder does not mean that we can't change. It just means that we may have more obstacles to overcome than other people do. These obstacles shut our mind to God's power and add to our own destruction. If we respond this way to any behavior, we need to admit our doubts and struggles and seek help in surrendering to God's will.

As we follow the principles of the Twelve Steps, we gradually and unconsciously prepare to have our shortcomings removed. We may realize that we are behaving differently—that we have changed. It is not unusual for others see the changes before we do. Worriers appear less anxious and fearful. Procrastinators learn to seek help from others to prioritize their work. Isolators start accepting invitations to social gatherings, and feel more at

> Don't quit five minutes before the miracle happens. Remember that change is a process—not an event. It takes time, and needs to be done according to God's schedule. When you feel impatient or discouraged and think there is no progress, that's when God is working the hardest.

ease speaking to others in a group setting. Leaders learn to use their talents in a way that is not controlling and in a way that empowers them to achieve their true potential. The need to kill the pain with chemicals, alcohol, activity, stimulation, sex, gambling, etc. decreases. People who diligently work the Steps as an integral part of their lives become calmer, more serene, and genuinely happy.

We have been "as sick as our secrets," and now we are as well as our honesty will allow us to be. Talking openly about our resentments, fears, and the harm we have done takes away their power to control our lives and can give us a sense of peace. Being honest to God, to ourselves, and to others will keep our hearts and spirits open to God's will and unconditional love. We will be able to focus our energy on developing the positive aspects of our ADD, rather than being in a constant state of panic, waiting for the next crisis.

A radiant, confident, and gifted person lives in each of us. Our wonderful qualities, however, are often hidden under a cloud of low self-esteem. If someone asked us if we wanted to be freed from the behaviors and traits that get us in trouble, we could give only one answer—Yes! We are entirely ready to have them removed. ADD and its symptoms are bad enough; when added to our other problem behavior, they drain our lives of joy and its meaning. We are indeed ready to know new freedom, peace, and sanity.

> *People may see your communication as disjointed, scattered, or incomplete. "Ready, shoot, aim!" or "Ready, speak, think!" is your standard way of processing things. You may start a sentence, then your brain gets ahead of your mouth, and you start a new sentence on a completely different subject. Create a win-win situation by asking people to tell you if they're confused. Your communication skills will improve, and people will be able to understand you.*

Having completed Step Six, we are ready to ask God to remove our character defects, and we look forward to replacing them with positive qualities. Many of us are just now beginning to identify some of our untapped, undeveloped abilities, and the adventure can be an exciting one.

 ## Key Ideas

Readiness: Step Six is the time when we prepare ourselves to let go of our character defects. We know the truth about ourselves, and we know our faults. Now we must become ready to let go of the faults so we can proceed with our recovery. If not, we won't be prepared for Step Seven, where we ask God to remove our shortcomings.

Character defects: Our character defects are the objectionable behaviors we developed to survive in our chaotic world. They are tools we began using in childhood and have built into our personalities. They are a part of who we are. This undesirable part of our nature must now be removed and replaced with godly character.

Willingness: Willingness is a state of mind that propels us into action. We may have the best intentions to do something, but until we are willing to act, nothing will happen. In Step Six, all of our good intentions simmer and brew until, with God's help, we are entirely ready and willing to commit ourselves to change.

Prayer for Step Six

Quiet my heart, God,
From all the activity and noise.
Help me center my thoughts, my mind.
Remove the distractions that spin me.
My wrongs, my faults lie before you.
You know me inside out, the good and the bad.
Help me receive your inner working and change.
I want to turn my back on yesterday's ways.
I want to truly desire change, lasting change.
So quiet my heart, make me ready.

REVIEW OF CHARACTER DEFECTS

Character defect	How it affects me and others
Anger	
Co-dependency	
Defiance	
Dishonesty	
Disrespect	
Envy	
Impatience	
Impulsivity	
Irresponsibility	
Lust	
Manipulation	
Selfishness	
Other	

This exercise will help you become ready to let go of the character defects you discovered when working Steps Four and Five. It is helpful to refer to your Step Four inventory when completing this exercise.

Why I resist having it removed	How my life will be better when it is removed

I'm interested in how you are doing since
you started a twelve-step program.
Write down how you are feeling and
what you are doing to take care of
yourself, so we can talk about it
next time I see you.

Step Six Review

The task of removing our objectionable behavior is more than we can handle alone. **Step Six** does not require that we do the removing; all we have to do is be "entirely ready" for it to happen. We can become ready by faithfully working the Steps and being willing to let our Higher Power help us remove our shortcomings. The character traits we want to eliminate are often deeply ingrained patterns of behavior—they will not vanish overnight. We must be patient while our Higher Power shapes us into new people. Allowing God to be in control helps us to trust more completely.

❑ Which character defects have caused you the most pain, and need to be removed first?

❑ Which character defects do you prefer to keep? Explain why you are still so attached to them.

❑ What is some of the negative self-talk that makes you think you will never be different?

❑ What does being "entirely ready" mean to you?

7

UNDERSTANDING STEP SEVEN

Anyone who has been seriously ill or injured knows what it's like to need others. It's a humbling experience to lie in bed and be unable to move or care for oneself. Even the simplest of needs must be met by others. By the time we come to Step Seven, we realize that we are on a sickbed, and we need God's help to get well. So far, each step has reinforced the fact that "We can't, but God can." We've given up the illusion that we can help ourselves. Our wounded past has caught up with us, and it's time to humble ourselves and ask for healing. We accomplish this by asking God to remove our shortcomings.

WORKING STEP SEVEN

Step Seven requires prayer. We work this step on our knees. Our condition, our honesty, and our pain have humbled us to the point where we must open our mouths and pray. It's tempting to pray in a general way, to ask God to remove everything as if it were a package deal. But that's not how the program works. In Step Four, we listed each character defect separately. In Step Five, we admitted our wrongs item by item. Step Seven is no different; we ask in humble prayer for the removal of our shortcomings—one defect at a time.

PREPARING FOR STEP SEVEN

We prepare for Step Seven by holding nothing back from God—there's no longer a glimmer of hope that we can control things on our own. If we successfully completed Step Six, we have become ready to let go of our defects. In Step Seven we draw closer to God by taking prayer seriously and recognizing its importance in our lives. This is a time to talk to our Higher Power in a very personal way about our moral inventory and the changes we want to make in our lives.

STEP SEVEN

Humbly asked God to remove our shortcomings.

Praying is no easy matter. It demands a relationship in which you allow someone other than yourself to enter into the very center of your being, and to see there what you would rather leave in darkness, to touch there what you would rather leave untouched.—HENRY NOUWEN

Humility is a foundation principle of the twelve-step program. Humility has helped us admit our powerlessness, freed us to believe in a Power greater than ourselves, and enabled us to turn our lives over to God's care. Now, in Step Seven, humility allows us to invite God to remove the shortcomings and character defects that have kept us from serenity and trust. From now on, humility will keep us from falling into the trap of self-reliance, and give us the compassion we need to be concerned for others.

The humility gained in this program opens our eyes to see that there are things more important than material security, personal ambition, and the gratification of all our needs. Humility opens our eyes and allows us to see that character building and spiritual values are the objectives that make life worth living and sharing.

I'm learning a lot more about love, patience, and tolerance for myself and others. I don't allow others to "push my buttons" so much anymore. By practicing humility, I can see the value of another person's opinion, and still respect the value of my own.

Sam's Story

"Sam! Turn off that damn computer and do what I told you!"

"I can't, Dad. I'm on the Internet. I'm the host of three different IRCs," Sam answered without looking up. . . . "Hey! What happened?"

"I turned off the power!" Dad barked.

"You butthead! You wrecked my computer. You're *never* supposed to turn the power off when. . . . "

"I'll wreck more than your computer if you don't do what I told you to do!" Dad shouted and charged at Sam. "And don't you *ever* call me a butthead again!"

"What did you tell me to do?" Sam pleaded to stop his father's rage.

"I told you to clean the garage," Dad answered—still angry enough to strike. "And I've been telling you to clean it for three weeks."

"Well, I haven't had the time," Sam countered.

"What? Like hell you haven't!" Dad reignited. "You've had time to play on the Internet and host IRCs. You should've thought about your responsibilities before you turned on that damn computer."

"I'm really busy," Sam shrugged.

"Too busy to do your chores? Too busy to obey you parents? Too busy to earn your keep? Listen, mister, if you're gonna live under this roof, you're gonna play by my rules. Do you understand?"

"Sure, Dad, whatever you say," Sam answered indifferently. He lifted his eyes off the floor long enough to see his mother standing in the hall. As usual she said nothing, but held her arms close over her stomach, and chewed on her bottom lip.

"Sam, if you haven't started to clean that garage by three this afternoon, you're gone. You're old enough to move out, and maybe it's time. Living on your own might teach you some responsibility!" And with that Dad slammed the bedroom door.

Sam took a deep breath. He held still and listened through the wall as his mom pleaded for patience and understanding. But Sam's dad lashed out with all the reasons why he thought Sam was worthless and lazy.

The thought of leaving home frightened Sam, but he couldn't keep counting on his mom to rescue him. Maybe it *is* time to move out, he thought. Try as he might, when the power came on and his computer rebooted, Sam felt paralyzed. *No way* could he obey his dad—it wasn't anywhere in his will or mood. Instead, he reached for the mouse, heard the modem dial the number, and lost himself in the only place where he could be somebody.

> *Often both father and son will have ADD, but only the son will be diagnosed. The father will have all the symptoms but will deny the possibility that he could have the disorder. He relies on angry outbursts, punishment, and shaming in an attempt to control, change, and motivate the son who is so much like himself. Unfortunately, the son develops low self-esteem and adopts behavior that will plague him in adulthood.*

Before, when pride blinded us, we falsely believed that we had to survive by relying solely on our individual strength and intelligence. We developed the philosophy that "If it has to be, it's up to me." We were afraid of feeling inadequate, afraid of being told that we are stupid or lazy, or worried about falling short of our expectations. We were often unhappy, frustrated, or angry. We rarely felt satisfied, even if we accomplished an important task. Our pride and self-reliance made it impossible for us to know God. Our pain and frustration opened a new door for us and shut the door on pride.

The result of our objectionable behavior and our futile attempts to change ourselves and others forced us to learn something about humility. Today we know that the basic ingredient of humility is the desire to seek and to do God's will rather than our own. God's will brings rest and peace. We know now that God will provide for our needs and desires according to a higher plan and purpose—that God's timing is perfect.

> *I'm tired of carrying around the baggage that reminds me of my parents and teachers telling me I was "bad." With the Twelve Steps as a guide, I can leave my old baggage behind and enjoy the journey ahead of me.*

Step Seven brings us to the threshold of a new life of rest, serenity, and peace. We want with all our hearts to leave our present life and its pain behind us, but many of us have old baggage that can't make the journey with us. Our Higher Power, the journey's host, is there to assure us that our valuable possessions are safely stowed and that anything we need will be provided. It's just the old, weighty, and corrupt things that can't make the trip. Like keeping a favorite suit or dress, we want to hang on to certain survival skills and character defects. We're not sure what life would be like without them. Like taking a weapon with us for protection, we want to take our trusted behaviors for protection. But our Higher Power says, "No. You're on a journey to a new life, and you won't need those old and worthless things."

It's important that we understand the power of giving up. What and how much we are willing to give up determines the type and degree of change that will occur. In the midst of troubling and painful situations, we used to look for what we could get or change to feel better. Now, we ask ourselves what is it that we need to give up, and how willing we are to do so. Our first response is to protect ourselves with familiar survival skills and take control. If we do this, we put God out of the picture, and we are far from serenity. It is better to recognize the old character defect and ask God to remove it.

> *Avoid tasks that make you feel overwhelmed and afraid of failure. Divide your tasks, like removal of your shortcomings, into bite-size pieces that can be accomplished within a reasonable amount of time. Doing this makes jobs more appealing, and you will find yourself more productive. Remember: Life is a trial, mile by mile. Life is hard, yard by yard. But life is a cinch, inch by inch!*

When you get rid of a character defect, you overcome a shortcoming. It's practically automatic. By nature's law, there is no void in the universe—something rushes in to fill it. So if we're willing to let go of a defect, something will appear in its place. With our commitment to live a better life with God's help, we can be confident that the void will be filled with something good. Fear will be replaced with courage; resentment with love, tolerance, and patience; pride with humility. Giving up our defects and shortcomings is like a balancing act. When we're long on fear, we're short on courage. When we're long on love, tolerance, and patience, we're short on resentments.

Step Seven directs us to ask for removal of all our shortcomings. But the process will be more manageable if we work on the easiest ones first to build up our confidence and strength. God will see that we achieve our goal at a pace that is comfortable for us. Our willingness to accept God's help builds trust and confidence in ourselves and in our Higher Power. Remember: praying for the removal of shortcomings doesn't mean we do the removing. We trust God to make the changes. For now, we simply pray and use our moral inventory as our guide for Step Seven.

We may find that after we ask God to relieve us of a burdensome behavior, it doesn't seem to go away. Anger or discouragement is understandable but self-defeating. It is more productive to reach out and ask for prayer support from a sponsor, coach, or a friend in recovery. It helps to express our negative feelings in prayer, knowing that our Higher Power understands. When things do not seem to go according to our timetable, reciting the Serenity Prayer can help.

Consider planning a going-away party or memorial service for your shortcomings. It doesn't have to be a real party, but it should be a memorable event that allows you to let go and say goodbye. One idea is to make a ceremony of burning your list of shortcomings and character defects. After burning the list, scatter the ashes, or commit them to the deep. Remember, you can't take them with you!

We have the right to express our own attitudes and feelings about what other people say or do to us. We can respond to them, but we don't need to react according to their expectations. In the same way, it's not our place to change or control another person. For example, someone might come up to us full of resentment and anger and say, "I want to set you straight! I don't like the way you. . . ." In the past, we might have defended ourselves, made excuses, or lashed out at the other person. Now, with a new measure of humility and trust, we can respond without feeling threatened. We can change the game and play according to our rules—not theirs. We can see the value of the other person's opinion and grow from it. We can also see the truth about the other person, and let a sick person be sick by showing compassion, patience, and love. The point is that we can't change the situation or the other person, but we can change our response to it!

As we notice our defects being removed, we must proceed with caution and guard against pride. Sudden changes in our behavior can and do happen, but we cannot anticipate them or direct them. God initiates change when we are ready, and we cannot claim that we alone removed

Recovery does not depend on willpower or self-discipline. It depends on your willingness to practice humility and invite God to guide you along the proper path. There is nothing God cannot fix if you come to God in humility.

our character defects. When we learn to ask humbly for God's help in our lives, change becomes God's responsibility. We cannot accept the credit, but we can give thanks.

Troublesome behaviors that remain after we complete Step Seven may never be eliminated, but we have an opportunity to transform these aspects of our character into positive traits. Leaders may be left with a quest for power, but will respect the abilities and limitations of others. Our impulsive nature will still be there, but we will use it to nurture our creative and intuitive side. With the help of our Higher Power, all aspects of our personal lives can be rewarding and fulfilling. By continuing to practice humility and accept the tools God gives us, we will eventually begin to aspire to a more peaceful life, sharing with others the love we have received.

We need to acknowledge ourselves for our commitment to recovery. Our desire and determination to change enabled us to break the bonds of unhealthy habits and behavior. Our courage to face the consequences freed us to be more accepting of our ADD characteristics. We accept the positive, spontaneous thoughts and feelings that occur, and see that they result from our personal relationship with God. We learn that the guidance we receive from our Higher Power is always available. All we need to do is listen, receive, and act without fear.

God removes your shortcomings and often provides strength and insight through other people. Teachers, ministers, medical doctors, and therapists can all be instruments of your Higher Power's work. Remember to take care of yourself physically, so that you will be mentally ready for the challenges in Step Seven.

 **Key Ideas**

Humility: Many of us misunderstand humility. It does not mean putting ourselves in second place and doing more for others. Humility does not mean saying we're sorry. Humility is seeing ourselves as God sees us. It is putting ourselves in proper perspective in light of God's plan. The basic ingredient of all humility is a desire to seek and to do God's will.

Giving up: Giving up is a variation of letting go—a way to release our shortcomings as God reveals them to us. We identify the things we need to eliminate, then release them to God. When we actually "give up" a character defect, we conquer a shortcoming.

Shortcomings: Shortcomings are the objectionable behaviors, character defects, and self-defeating attitudes that have been revealed to us through the Steps. We have been working on our shortcomings for three Steps now. In Step Four we listed them; in Step Five we admitted them; in Step Six we became ready to have God remove them. Now, in Step Seven, we humbly ask God to remove them.

Prayer for Step Seven

God, grant me the grace to surrender,
So I can have peace for today.
Take away my fears and worries.
Give me faith that all is okay.

You know my need to fret, to fear.
You know I always expect the worst.
I need more faith, more confidence,
To know your power is at work.

Today you have a plan for me,
And I know your plan is best.
So if I drift or wander or stray,
Draw me back to your loving nest.

Keep me focused on your presence.
Keep me full of joy and light.
Your plan for me is always best.
And your ways are always right.

Today, I'll watch your plan unfold.
I will remember that you're working.
I'll reject the urge to brood and fret,
And find true peace in trusting.

REMOVAL OF SHORTCOMINGS

Shortcoming	Replacement
Anger	Kindness
Co-dependency	Interdependency
Defiance	Submission
Dishonesty	Honor
Disrespect	Reverence
Envy	Charity
Impatience	Patience
Impulsivity	Planning
Irresponsibility	Dependability
Lust	Moderation
Manipulation	Trust
Selfishness	Generosity
Other	

This exercise will help you become ready to let go of the character defects you discovered when working Steps Four and Five. It is helpful to refer to your Step Four inventory when completing this exercise.

How I am behaving differently	How my life is better

Now that you have completed Step Seven, make a list of how the Twelve Steps are helping you in your journey. What special benefits are you gaining from the Steps?

STEP SEVEN REVIEW

Humility is the central theme of **Step Seven.** By practicing humility we receive the strength necessary to work the Steps and achieve satisfactory results. We recognize that a major portion of our lives has been devoted to fulfilling our self-centered desires. We must set aside these prideful, selfish behavior patterns and realize that humility frees our spirit. Step Seven requires surrendering our will to our Higher Power so that we may receive the serenity we need to achieve happiness.

❏ How are you benefiting from God's presence in your life?

❏ List some of your "easier" shortcomings that you can ask God to remove right now.

❏ List examples that indicate you are practicing humility.

❏ Which of your negative character traits are becoming positive? What changes do you see?

8

UNDERSTANDING STEP EIGHT

As kids, we loved to blame others for our behavior, and to deny our own responsibility. Our parents tried their best to make us feel responsible and apologize. But we were not willing to say "I'm sorry. I was out of line." It was too much of an affirmation that we were "bad."

In Step Eight we begin to grow up and take responsibility for our actions without concerning ourselves about the wrongs done to us. Although we were hurt by others who did not understand our behavior, this Step is for our healing, not theirs.

In the first seven Steps we dealt with our own situation. Steps Four and Five were our inventory and our admissions—nobody else's. In Step Eight we look at how our behavior caused harm to others. It is now that we consider the people we harmed.

WORKING STEP EIGHT

Step Eight involves thoughtful reflection. With God's help, we recall the names and faces of people we have harmed, write down their names, and consider each person carefully. We began the process in Step Four when we listed our resentments and fears and the harms we have done. In Step Eight we examine our relationships with these people and determine how we hurt them.

PREPARING FOR STEP EIGHT

We prepare for Step Eight through practicing humility and becoming willing to confront our past and make restitution. It requires that we recognize our part in the harm done to others. It will be easier to complete Step Eight if we make room in our busy schedule for quiet time and reflection. This can be done by attending a retreat or going to a favorite hideaway for a few days.

STEP EIGHT

Made a list of all persons we had harmed, and became willing to make amends to them all.

There is no way God can control our minds when our minds are being dominated by something that occurred in the past. Our only way to get rid of these blocks is to clear them up. —JOE MCQ, *THE STEPS WE TOOK*

Until we began working the Steps, our lives were not our own. Our resentments and fears toward others had occupied our minds and controlled our thoughts. In a sort of knee-jerk reaction, we were constantly bouncing around, trying to manage our ADD symptoms, make ourselves acceptable to others, and live with the negative tapes that constantly reminded us of our inabilities and inconsistencies. We had lost our lives to the guilt and remorse that plagued us because of our shameful behavior toward others and the harm we had done to them.

The guilt and remorse that linger because of harm done to others will not fully release their grip upon us until we make amends for our past wrongdoings. To become free, we must look back at the instances that cause us guilt and remorse, and attempt to repair the damage. Our inventory revealed many of the

> It isn't the load that weighs you down, it's the way you carry it. Take responsibility for your actions and be willing to make amends for your wrongs. Resolving the guilt and remorse will make your burden lighter.

behaviors that caused injury to ourselves and others. In Step Eight we begin by accepting full responsibility for our own behavior and being willing to make amends.

Carl's Story

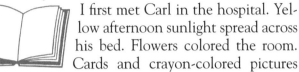 I first met Carl in the hospital. Yellow afternoon sunlight spread across his bed. Flowers colored the room. Cards and crayon-colored pictures filled a corkboard and announced that this man was loved. But Carl didn't seem to feel the warmth of the sun, see the color, or know the love. His eyes darted around the room following phantoms. His arms tugged and fought the restraints.

I pulled up a chair and introduced myself. Carl didn't turn to acknowledge me, but spoke as if we were in the middle of a conversation. "You know, Jerry, I don't have anything going for me. I look at my life, my forty-plus years, and I don't have a damn thing to show for it."

"What do you mean?"

As I asked, Carl turned. He searched my face as if he'd just noticed me, and answered, "Just what I said. I don't have anything to be proud of. I've never had a real career—only lots of meaningless jobs. I've never been a success at anything. I don't own a house. I have debts, not savings. No retirement. Others have friends, not me. And since my divorce, I don't even have a family."

I found it hard to see the pain and sadness in Carl's eyes. He was so intense it frightened me. He continued, "You know what my problem is?" I prayed that his question was rhetorical, because I had no clue. "My problem is that I've got a sign on my ass that says 'Kick me!' You see it, don't you?"

I gulped and said the only thing that came to mind. "What do you mean?"

"I mean, I seem to invite the whole world to abuse me. Why else would everybody kick me around and take advantage of me they way they do, then leave me with nothing but bruises to show for my hard work and trouble? Huh?"

As Carl looked at me his face became softer—settled. I think he finally realized that a real person was next to him. "You know, they think my car wreck below Point Mugu was a suicide attempt. But I'll tell ya, if I wanted to kill myself, I would. But I'm too chicken. I just drive fast when I'm hurting. I love the rush, and I like cruising the coast when I need to think. I just couldn't hold the curve." Carl paused and studied my face. "I'll bet you think I'm crazy."

"No, I really don't," I answered. "I think you're confused, not crazy. I know what you mean about having nothing and feeling like nobody."

"Really?"

"Yeah. And for years I blamed everything and everyone in my life for all my problems. I never could accept the idea that my problems had anything to do with how I behaved."

"What changed to make you feel different?" Carl asked.

"It wasn't *what* changed; it was *who*," I said. "*I* changed."

The friend who asked me to visit Carl had said it might be a twelve-step call on a fellow ADDer. She was right. Carl's psychiatrist later confirmed that Carl did have ADD, just as his ex-wife suspected. That day, and in days that followed, I shared my story with Carl. I told him about my ADD, the Twelve Steps, and the changes I had experienced. I told him I used to have the same "Kick me!" sign that invited so many troubles. I told Carl how I'm amazed at the miracle of the Steps and the power they have to bring us back to people and to love.

> *Learning to deal with my resentments and fears is helping me to interact better with others. I don't waste time trying to get even, so I have more time to spend on getting ahead.*

If we have thoroughly worked the first seven Steps, we are now experiencing a new freedom. We know what it's like to be released from the bondage of resentment and fear. We know what it's like to humbly and honestly respond to others, speaking the truth in love instead of acting out of self-will. We're learning to patiently accept God's timing and will for the outcome of things. We know a new peace and serenity that comes from trusting our Higher Power. But we are not yet entirely free. We have one last hurdle to overcome—that of forgiveness.

Step Eight begins the process of healing damaged relationships through our willingness to make amends for past misdeeds. We can let go of our resentments and fears and start to overcome the guilt, shame, and remorse we have because of our harmful actions. We can leave behind the gray, angry world of loneliness and move toward a bright future by being willing to make things right. The gifts of God's love and the Twelve Steps are all the tools we need to overcome past wreckage and mend our broken relationships.

To consider harm done to others, we must examine our past relationships, many of which carry painful memories. We might

> *Program members will tell you that the best place to start making amends is to change your behavior. If structure is a problem for you, and if your scattered thinking causes problems for others, ask someone to help you create some structure in your life. You will benefit from the structure, and the people who are bothered by your behavior will see and appreciate your efforts to change.*

be tempted to say, "That's water under the bridge!" "That's better left forgotten." Or "Hey, nobody is perfect." But healing requires that we face our part in the problem. It's time to stop blaming others for mistreating us and to prepare to make amends for our wrongs. Just because our problems stem from a condition over which we have no control doesn't give us the right to take it out on others. The idea that "They hurt me more than I ever hurt them" doesn't work anymore. This is our Step Eight, and we are required to focus on the hurt we inflicted upon others. What they did to us is their business. Whether or not they ask for our forgiveness is not our problem. Our relief will come in Step Nine when we make amends and thereby forgive ourselves.

> *Unwillingness to forgive can powerfully affect you both physically and emotionally. The energy you use to hold grudges and keep track of wrongs done to you would be better spent doing something to take care of yourself. Try to forgive. You'll feel better and look better.*

The first part of Step Eight requires only that we make a list of the people whom we have harmed. We don't have to take any other action. If we did our inventory correctly, we listed our resentments, fears, and harmful actions, and analyzed them. In reviewing our inventory, we saw where we hurt some of the people we resented and feared. These names begin the list that we will use to make our amends in Step Nine. In addition to these names, we need to list any other people we have harmed in any way. When completing the list of amends, we will see the harms we have done, and we'll be able to take sincere and beneficial action to clear things up.

When thinking about the people we have harmed, we see how our ADD-related behavior and our character defects have

Use symbols and sayings as a quick way to cope
with your ADD traits. When you turn left
instead of right and take your family on a 20-
minute detour, it is better to be able to say,
"There goes my ADD again," than to argue
that you didn't do it on purpose. Ask family
members to give you clues when your ADD
causes them frustration. They could say "Poof!" as a loving
hint that you tuned out and stopped paying attention.

played a major part in sabotaging our lives and our relationships. For example:

■ When we became angry, we often hurt ourselves more than
others. This may have caused feelings of depression or self-pity.
■ Persistent financial problems resulting from our impulsiveness or irresponsible actions caused trouble with family and
creditors.
■ When confronted with an issue about which we felt guilty,
we lashed out at others instead of looking honestly at ourselves.
■ Frustrated by our lack of control, we behaved aggressively
and intimidated those around us.
■ Because of our indiscriminate sexual behavior, true intimacy
was impossible to achieve or maintain.
■ Our need to cling to others for direction and supervision
sometimes hurt our relationships, because we expected others
to tell us what to do. We became dependent on them, and they
felt smothered by our neediness.

Step Eight asks that we look at our behavior and become
willing to make amends for the wrongs we committed. We
must be prepared to accept the consequences and take whatever measures are necessary to make amends. This means
acknowledging our part in a situation where someone was
harmed. Accepting responsibility and making appropriate
restitution are vitally important. Only by expressing genuine
regret for our behavior can we complete the housecleaning

necessary for putting the past behind us and achieving the peace and serenity we desire.

Making amends is a difficult task—one that we will execute with increasing skill, yet never really finish. Again, uncomfortable feelings may surface as we recognize the damage our actions have caused. To repair our past wrongdoings, we must be willing to face them. When preparing the list of people we have harmed, it is best to keep our thoughts directed toward making things right. Although our intentions may be rebuffed, our desire is to obey God and find healing. People on our list may feel bitter toward us and resist our attempts at restitution. They may hold deep grudges and be unwilling to reconcile with us. No matter how we are received, we must be willing to proceed. The amends we make are for our own benefit, not the benefit of those we have harmed.

Many of the symptoms that are common to people with ADD can sabotage relationships. The symptoms themselves will not go away, but as you learn to live with ADD you can modify your behavior. It is crucial that you understand the difference between the symptoms you inherited and the character defects you developed. The symptoms can't change, but the behavior can! Your job is to know the difference.

Occasionally we will not be able to directly face the people on our list. They may be deceased, separated from us, or unwilling to meet with us. Whatever the situation, we still need to put them on our list. When we make the amends in Step Nine, we will see why amends are necessary, even if they cannot be made face to face. Being willing to make them will release us from hard feelings and help us find serenity and peace of mind.

When making our list of people, we must remember to focus on ourselves. We are all victims of self-inflicted pain

I'm adding fun to my life and relationships by using funstarters— allowing myself to have fun. I'm also getting rid of my fun-blocks—whatever keeps me from having fun. As a fun-seeker—I'm discovering my own fun and being honest about what is fun for ME!

because we did not have the skills to deal with our ADD appropriately. We spent time and energy trying to fit in and pass for normal, instead of being who God made us to be. We sacrificed ourselves in the process. We may have been our own worst enemy and experienced excessive self-blame, guilt, and shame. Taking time to look at the harm we have inflicted upon ourselves and being willing to forgive ourselves is essential to our continued growth.

In Step Nine, we will seek out the people whom we have harmed, and make amends wherever necessary. For now, all we need to do is list them and describe our harmful behavior. Our actions may have caused emotional, financial, or physical pain for others. We need to take as much time as necessary to reflect on our list and to be as thorough as possible. Being totally honest with ourselves is a major factor in our ability to make restitution for our past destructive actions.

Key Ideas

Amends: Within the context of the Twelve Steps, the idea of making amends is broadly defined as "repairing the damage of the past." The process can be as simple as apologizing or as complex as making restitution for physical or financial liability.

Forgiveness: Forgiveness is a decision, not an emotion. It comes when we stop feeling resentful of people who we think have harmed us. True forgiveness is accomplished only with God's help. Our Higher Power alone can give us the grace, desire, and ability to release those who have hurt us. When we list the people we have harmed, we immediately think about how others have harmed us. This reaction is a defense mechanism—a way to avoid admitting our own guilt. It doesn't matter why we feel this way; what matters is that we deal with it and forgive those who have hurt us. Left to ourselves, we allow bitterness and resentment to fester.

 ## *Prayer for Step Eight*

Higher Power, I ask your help
In listing all those I have harmed.
I will take responsibility for my mistakes,
And be forgiving to others as you are forgiving to me.
Grant me the willingness to begin my restitution.
This I pray.

PREPARING TO MAKE AMENDS

This exercise will help you list the people you have harmed, and prepare you for actually making amends in Step Nine. Be as thorough as possible in listing the names of all those who have been affected by your hurtful behavior.

	Who I hurt	Relation to me	What I did	How it hurt the person	How it hurt me
	John	husband	I insulted him	He was embarrassed	I felt guilty
1					
2					
3					
4					
5					
6					
7					
8					
9					

STEP EIGHT REVIEW

Step Eight begins the process of healing damaged relationships through our willingness to make amends for past misdeeds. We prepare ourselves to carry out our Higher Power's master plan for our lives by getting ready to make amends. We can let go of our resentments and fears and start to overcome the guilt, shame, and low self-esteem we have acquired through our harmful behavior.

❏ List three personal experiences that require making amends.

❏ About which relationship do you feel the greatest resentment, fear, guilt, or shame? Explain.

❏ Why is forgiving yourself an important factor in the amends-making process?

❏ How has the quality of your life improved since beginning your twelve-step work?

9

UNDERSTANDING STEP NINE

Natural disasters like earthquakes, hurricanes, fires, and floods capture our attention. They receive major coverage, but rarely do we have a chance to see the hard work of rebuilding that takes place after the disaster has past. Lives, homes, businesses, and whole communities are repaired and revived. As observers, we are not affected the way we would be if the tragedy had happened to us. Step Nine is similar to the rebuilding that takes place after a disaster. In Step Eight we surveyed the damage. Now we go into action. Through the process of making amends, we make restitution and repair the damage of our past.

WORKING STEP NINE

Working Step Nine involves making direct amends to those we have harmed. We approach each one we can with gentleness, sensitivity, and understanding. Our Higher Power will help us to know the best way to make contact. Making amends to some people will require a face-to-face meeting, while other situations may be handled simply by changing our behavior. In some cases, making direct amends will not be possible because of circumstances beyond our control. Whatever the case, God will give us the wisdom and direction we need.

PREPARING FOR STEP NINE

We prepare for Step Nine by making our amends list as complete as possible. We should include ourselves on the list and be prepared to make personal amends. We review our list from Step Eight and determine the best way to make contact with each person. There is no need to hurry. The important thing is that we are willing to make amends. God will give us special insight and direction and help us overcome any fear or apprehension that may arise.

STEP NINE

Made direct amends to such people wherever possible, except when to do so would injure them or others.

The unfinished friendships of this life are at once its dearest experiences and most glorious of hopes. —ELIZABETH STUART PHELPS

Most of us have accidentally left an ingredient out of a recipe. Even something as seemingly insignificant as baking soda can result in a flat cake. Or maybe we omitted a tiny pinch of salt and made our morning oatmeal taste like paste. We learned from experience that it is impossible to go back and replace the missing ingredient. It had to be applied at the right time in the process. The Twelve Steps, like a recipe, require certain ingredients at the proper time. And now it is time to add the important ingredient of Step Nine if we want good results. If we don't include Step Nine in full measure, we won't find release from the guilt and remorse that result from harm done to others.

> *Step Nine requires input and wisdom from a sponsor who is familiar with the Steps. This Step involves making decisions that may affect some relationships for the rest of your life. During her Step Nine work, one woman asked her sponsor if she could make amends by mail. The sponsor said, "Sure—if the harm was done by mail."*

If we have worked Steps One through Seven correctly and then choose to skip over Step Nine, we will lose the ground we've gained. Our resentments and fears will return and occupy our minds, thus keeping us from doing God's will. Again we will avoid the people we resent and fear, hide from the ones to whom we owe money, and go back to blaming others for our problems. We will run the risk of reversing the decision we made in Step Three to turn our lives over to God's care. There's a good chance we will revert to our "self-will run riot" behavior and have to return to Step Three.

Jim's Story

"Hello?"
"I quit! I'm not gonna do this amends crap!"
"Jim, is that you?"
"This is for the birds! It's *gotta* be some sadist's view of a good time, and I think it sucks! I'm doing a great job working the Steps, but *this* stuff is downright abusive. I don't need the grief."

"Jim, when you asked me to sponsor you, you said you needed someone to keep you on track. You wanted me to help you muster the courage to make your amends. I do my part, but I need your help."

"You don't get it! It's not *my* problem. It's those pinheads who used to work for me! They're using this amends crap to make me feel bad 'cause I made something of my life. Can I help it if they're poor?"

"Okay, Jim, I get it. Tell me what happened. Who did you try to make amends to?"

"Kim, a girl who used to work for me in the remodeling end of the business," Jim answered. "She did sales and customer follow-up—stuff like that."

"Good. What did you say to her?"

"Well, before I told her about this ADD thing and the amends baloney, I just wanted to make small talk. So I asked her about her daughter."

"Good. Then what?"

"So she told me that after I let her go, the bum who lived with her moved out. Then she started whining about no medical insurance and her daughter's condition. . . . Hell, I don't remember. All I know is that she started to dump on me something fierce."

"Then what, Jim?"

"Well, I couldn't take it. I blew up. I told her she wouldn't be so bad off if she'd worked harder and spent less time criticizing and telling me off."

"What did she mean by that?"

"She was always raggin' on me about cash-flow problems. Who cares if payroll is a day or two late? She was always telling me I was too rough on the crew and clients. The crew was a bunch of lazy, good-for-nothing bums who couldn't keep up with me. All I wanted was to get in there, do the job, and get out. I couldn't care less about talkin' to some old lady who didn't know the difference between tile and texture. That was Kim's job. And I couldn't help it if the job cost more than her estimate."

"After you blew up . . . what happened then?"

"Well, she told me to leave. She said I was just as angry, abusive, and impatient as before. I said '*fine!*' and walked away. As I was leaving, she said, 'You know, Jim, I'm better off without your job. Even without medical insurance or money to buy food, I'm happier than I was before.'" Then Jim stopped talking.

There was a pause before Jim's sponsor said, "Thanks. I see what kind of man you are now."

"What?"

"I got to see that courage you said you had," the sponsor answered.

"Hey," Jim answered, "there's a big difference between courage and stupidity."

"You said it, Jim."

> *When I was at the height of my ADD craziness, I was very self-centered. I loved things and used people. The Steps are teaching me to value myself and others, and I'm starting to understand the importance of loving people and using things.*

To some degree, all of us are selfish and self-centered. We are so concerned about surviving and "passing for normal" that we focus too much on our own needs and sometimes don't give others the respect they deserve. We see people as objects to be used, and don't realize how we treat them. We end up running people off instead of recognizing their value and enjoying their company.

Having completed Steps Four through Nine, we see what we have done to harm people and cause them to shy away from us. We understand our behavior, and know that we have to make some changes in order to relate to others in a healthier way. Because we have more awareness of our ADD traits, it will be easier to make these changes. Step Nine is an opportunity to rebuild our lost relationships with others—to make amends for the behavior that offended them.

Step Nine will help us bridge the gap that exists between us and others because of our low opinion of ourselves, which caused us to withdraw from God and others. Our withdrawal was rarely a conscious act, but our return must be. We withdrew because we were overwhelmed, distracted, miserable, or afraid of being hurt. Our survival skills and self-will led us to believe that we were better off by taking care of ourselves and not relying on others. But our self-reliance only left us lonely and cut off from God and from others. In Step Nine we begin the process of rebuilding relationships by willingly interacting with others.

Making amends helps release us from many of the resentments and fears of our past. We achieve serenity in our lives by seeking forgiveness from those we have harmed and by making restitution where necessary. Without forgiveness, the resentments and fears will continue to undermine our growth and

> *Making schedules and setting priories is as important for social activities as it is for work. A big problem for people with ADD is that they don't take time for themselves—for the fun things in life. Make a sincere effort to take time for yourself. Success in recovery and in life requires that you schedule time for activities with friends. Adhere to these schedules faithfully.*

cause us stress. Making amends releases us from guilt and remorse and promotes freedom and health in mind and body.

If we ask for forgiveness but don't receive it, we must respond with understanding, knowing that it may take time, and because not everyone will believe that we can change. In any event, God knows what's in our hearts and gives us the forgiveness and acceptance we need.

The judgment, courage, stamina, and proper sense of timing we need for Step Nine are available from our Higher Power. God helps us choose the best way to make amends—either directly or indirectly. The process involves acknowledging the pain that others have endured because of our actions. We can only pray that God will prepare their hearts to receive our amends and forgive us. Beginning with the easy situations first helps us build confidence in our ability to succeed. Then, as making amends becomes more difficult, we will have more courage and feel more comfortable with our ability to make successful amends.

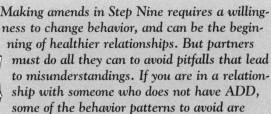

> *Making amends in Step Nine requires a willingness to change behavior, and can be the beginning of healthier relationships. But partners must do all they can to avoid pitfalls that lead to misunderstandings. If you are in a relationship with someone who does not have ADD, some of the behavior patterns to avoid are mess-maker and mess-cleaner-upper; pesterer and tuner-outer; victim and victimizer; master and slave.*

Some people may feel bitter toward us because of our ADD-related behavior rather than because of our character defects. For example, they may interpret our restlessness or inattentiveness as signals that we don't value their friendship. Some may feel offended because we don't keep in touch or return phone calls promptly. People may resent the burdens placed on them because of our disorganization, forgetfulness, incomplete communication, or procrastination. No matter what their reason is, we need to contact them and make amends. If someone does not know that we have ADD, or what it means, we can tell them about the disorder when we make the amends.

With all the stress and anxiety that can accompany the process of making amends, it is important to monitor your condition regularly. If you are taking medication, be sure to tell your doctor what you are doing. Your doctor will be able to talk with you about how you are feeling and how your medicine is working, and make recommendations for change when necessary. Don't be embarrassed to explain your situation to your doctor, who is there to help you manage your ADD symptoms effectively.

When working this Step, we need to distinguish between making amends and offering apologies. Apologies are appropriate, but they cannot substitute for making amends. A person can apologize for being late for work, but until the behavior is corrected, amends cannot be made. It is important to apologize when necessary, but it is more important to commit to changing the unacceptable behavior.

A number of stumbling blocks can hinder our progress in Step Nine. Two of these stumbling blocks are distractibility and procrastination. We know that making amends is important, but sometimes it is difficult to get started. Other more interesting things capture our attention and eat up our time. Another stumbling block is the sense of relief we feel because our lives are a lot less complicated than they were before we entered the program. We think our task is complete because we feel better. Denial may become a problem, because we don't want to risk the pain of facing people we have harmed. We may rationalize that the time isn't right, or that it's better to let bygones be bygones. Whatever the reason, it is important that we take a risk and begin the process.

Occasional emotional or spiritual relapses are to be expected and should be dealt with as promptly as possible. If not, they block our ability to make successful amends. When these relapses occur, we must accept them as signals that we are not working the Steps effectively. Perhaps we have turned away from God or stopped attending meetings. We may have eliminated something from our inventory and may need to refer back to Step Four. Or if we are unwilling to relinquish a self-defeating behavior, we need to return to Steps Six and Seven.

> *In Step Nine you will need all the support you can get from your sponsor, coach, or recovery partner. Supportive people can provide the stability and encouragement you need to stay on course. Keep a list of names and phone numbers handy, so contact will be easy when you need it most.*

Steps Eight and Nine help us repair the past and set the stage for a brighter future through improved relationships and a deeper awareness of the harm we have done to others. In these two Steps we take responsibility for hurting others, and we make restitution where we have inflicted harm. We have a chance to redeem ourselves for past misdeeds by making amends, and can look forward to a healthier and more rewarding future. Our self-esteem begins to improve, and we can achieve peaceful relations with God, ourselves, and others.

> *I made amends to my mom the other day. I was really scared, so I called my sponsor first. She reminded me that courage takes the place of fear, and tolerance takes the place of resentment. Her philosophy really worked. My mom thanked me, and told me she loves me. Making amends became very special for me when Mom asked me for forgiveness!*

By the time we have worked Steps Eight and Nine successfully, we are ready to experience The Promises. The action part of our journey is over, and we are ready to begin the continuation process which starts in Step Ten. These promises are what we have tried so hard to achieve, and have finally begun to enjoy. The Promises, on pages 83–84 in *Alcoholics Anonymous* (The Big Book) are:

- We are going to know a new freedom and a new happiness.
- We will not regret the past nor wish to shut the door on it.
- We will comprehend the word *serenity* and we will know peace.
- No matter how far down the scale we have gone, we will see how our experience can benefit others.
- That feeling of uselessness and self-pity will disappear.
- We will lose interest in selfish things and gain interest in our fellows.
- Self-seeking will slip away.
- Our whole attitude and outlook upon life will change.
- Fear of people and of economic insecurity will leave us.
- We will intuitively know how to handle situations that used to baffle us.
- We will suddenly realize that God is doing for us what we could not do for ourselves.

 **Key Ideas**

Direct amends: Direct amends are made personally to some-one we have harmed. We schedule an appointment and arrange to meet in person. If physical distance is a problem, we can talk on the phone or write a letter. The process includes telling them we are in a program that requires us to make amends. We request permission to make amends to them, and then make amends without placing any blame on them or others.

Indirect amends: Indirect amends are nonpersonal amends that we make to those we harmed. We make indirect amends to someone who is deceased, whose location is unknown, or who is inaccessible for another reason. Indirect amends also include those that cannot be made in person because they could harm others. These amends can be made by writing a letter we don't mail, by praying, or by doing a kindness to someone else, such as a family member of the person we have harmed.

Amends to self: The one person we often harm the most is ourselves. The process of making amends will not be complete unless we take time to set things right with ourselves. The best way to do this is to write a letter to ourselves and then read it while sitting in front of a mirror.

Prayer for Step Nine

Higher Power,
I pray for the right attitude to make my amends,
Being ever mindful not to harm others in the process.
I ask for your guidance in making indirect amends.
Most important, I will continue to make amends
By helping others, watching my behavior,
And growing spiritually.

STEP NINE EXERCISE

Making Amends

Believe me, every man has his secret sorrows,
which the world knows not, and oftimes we call a man cold,
when he is only sad.

—HENRY WADSWORTH LONGFELLOW

Step Nine has two distinct parts.

Made direct amends to such people wherever possible . . .

Direct amends include people who are accessible and who can be approached when we are ready. They include family members, friends, creditors, and co-workers. As part of making amends, we must try to repair the damage that has been done. If the damage involves a financial or material wrong, we must make a sincere effort to pay back what was taken. We may be surprised by how willing some people are to accept our amends, and, in turn, forgive us. We may even wonder why we waited so long to resolve the conflict.

Some circumstances will prevent us from making direct personal contact. These may involve people who are no longer accessible to us. In such cases, making indirect amends can satisfy our need for reconciliation. Indirect amends can be made by praying or by writing a letter as if we were actually communicating with the absent person. The important thing is that we make the contact necessary to satisfy our need to make amends. We also can make amends by performing a kindness for someone connected in some way to the person we harmed.

. . . except when to do so would injure them or others.

The process of making amends includes people to whom we can make only partial restitution because full disclosure could harm them or others. These people include spouses, ex-partners, former business associates, or friends. We must analyze the harm that could result if complete disclosure were made. This is especially true in cases of inappropriate sexual conduct, where all parties could be irreparably damaged if direct amends were made. If the matter has to be discussed to complete the process of making amends, talking to a trusted friend, coach, or sponsor is sufficient. Simply talking about the harm and admitting it to someone can remove our guilt and remorse and set us free.

Some amends should not be made directly because they could result in serious consequences to one or both parties. In cases involving potential loss of employment, imprisonment, or alienation from one's family, the consequences must be weighed carefully. If we delay making amends merely out of fear for ourselves or others, we will ultimately be the ones to suffer. In such situations, we can seek outside guidance from a counselor, minister, or close friend to decide on the best way to proceed. Otherwise we will delay our growth and stagnate, halting our progress toward a new and healthier life.

Some of our amends may require deferred action, so we must consider each situation carefully. It is seldom advisable to approach a person who still suffers deeply from the injustices we have done. In situations where our own pain is still deeply embedded, we may need more time for our own healing. In these cases, it is wise to seek counsel before taking any action. Proper timing is important, and we must be careful not to let our impulsive nature override our good judgment. Our ultimate goal is personal growth and reconciliation, and acting in haste without considering the consequences might create further injury.

Below are some guidelines to use in preparing for and making amends.

Have a good attitude toward making the amends.
▪ Be willing to love and forgive yourself and the other person.
▪ Take responsibility for what you are going to say and be willing to accept the consequences.
▪ Be careful not to blame the other person.

Prepare yourself.

▪ Devote time to prayer and meditation.

▪ Be sure that the timing is appropriate and that you are not acting impulsively.

▪ Keep it short and simple. Details and explanations aren't necessary.

Plan what you are going to say to the other person. For example:

_____, I'm here because I want you to know how _____ (scared, overwhelmed, abandoned, etc.) I was feeling when _____ happened between us. I know that I hurt you because _____ (harm done), and it's important to me that you know how much I regret what I did. I've probably done a lot of other things that I'm not aware of, and I'm sorry for those too. I ask for your forgiveness. I'm sincerely trying to behave in a more appropriate manner and stop hurting people.

or

_____, I'm here to make amends to you about _____. For all the words that I said out of (fear, thoughtlessness, anger, etc.) and confusion, I ask your forgiveness. I'm sincerely trying to behave better and stop hurting people.

Plan what you are going to say to yourself. For example:

I was _____ (scared, overwhelmed, feeling abandoned, etc.) when _____ happened. I forgive myself for the _____ (harm done) and anything else I may have done through my thoughts, words, or actions to cause myself harm.

MAKING AMENDS

Amends I plan to make now or later

	COLUMN 1 To whom	COLUMN 2 How I will make it	COLUMN 3 What I fear	COLUMN 4 When I made it	COLUMN 5 How it helped me
	Dad	*by phone*	*anger, rejection*	*Father's day*	*I feel less guilty*
1					
2					
3					
4					
5					
6					
7					
8					
9					

INSTRUCTIONS FOR COMPLETION

Column 1 Transfer the names from your list in Step Eight to one of the charts. Complete column 1 before going to column 2.

Column 2 List how you plan to make the amends (e.g., in person, by phone, by letter, by third party, by kindness to another, or by prayer) or how you would like to do it if it were possible.

Column 3 List your fears about the process. Complete column 3 before going to column 4.

Column 4 If amends can be made, list when you make them, and how they helped you.

Finally Use this worksheet to plan making your amends, and to record when you actually make amends. This may be a long and involved process, so don't get discouraged if you don't finish your list quickly.

Amends I may never make

	COLUMN 1 To whom	COLUMN 2 How I want to make it	COLUMN 3 What I fear	COLUMN 4 Why I may not make it	COLUMN 5 When I made it
	My boss	*in person*	*being fired*	*I can't afford to lose my job*	
1					
2					
3					
4					
5					
6					
7					
8					
9					

INSTRUCTIONS FOR COMPLETION

Column 1 Transfer the names from your list in Step Eight to one of the charts. Complete column 1 before going to column 2.

Column 2 List how you plan to make the amends (e.g., in person, by phone, by letter, by third party, by kindness to another, or by prayer) or how you would like to do it if it were possible. Complete column 2 before going to column 3.

Column 3 List your fears about the process. Complete column 3 before going to column 4.

Column 4 & 5 If amends can be made, list when you make them, and how they helped you. If making amends may not be possible, list what may prevent it. If you are able to make amends, indicate when you did it.

Finally Use this worksheet to plan making your amends, and to record when you actually make amends. This may be a long and involved process, so don't get discouraged if you don't finish your list quickly.

At this point, you deserve a pat on the back for your courage in getting this far. List the accomplishments for which you are most proud.

STEP NINE REVIEW

Step Nine fulfills our requirement to reconcile with others. We clear our "garden" of dead leaves and "rake up and discard" the old habits. We face our faults, admit our wrongs, and ask for forgiveness. Making amends will release us from many of the resentments and fears of our past. It is a means of achieving serenity in our lives by seeking forgiveness from those we have harmed and making restitution where necessary.

❏ How will making amends enable you to bury the past and improve your self-esteem?

❏ What difficulties are you having in making amends?

❏ Who on your amends list causes you the most anxiety? What is the reason for this anxiety?

❏ Who on your amends list do you consider to be an enemy? How do you plan to make amends to this person?

UNDERSTANDING STEP TEN

Anyone who has planted a garden knows the care required to keep it healthy. We must remove weeds, fertilize, bank the soil to hold water, plant the seeds, water, and guard against insects. It requires constant maintenance to keep the garden healthy.

Our recovery needs to be tended like a garden. Our lives were like the weeds. But God has helped us plant a healthy garden. God helped us pull the weeds and caused some wonderful things to grow in their place. We are beginning to see fruits of lasting change. But we also see the threat of weeds returning. As long as we live, those old self-reliant ways will try to recapture our lives. So we must continue to take personal inventory and protect our garden.

WORKING STEP TEN

Step Ten is a continuous practicing of Steps Four through Nine. Every day we take an inventory and admit what we find. We become willing to have our Higher Power change us, and then we humbly ask God to remove our shortcomings. We make note of the amends needed, and we make those amends. The new element is the nature of the inventory—the key word being *continued*. Step Ten is simply a continuous working of what we have already done in the previous Steps.

PREPARING FOR STEP TEN

We prepare for Step Ten by understanding that our defects will never completely go away, and we must watch for signs of their return. We do this by learning as much as we can about ourselves through the continuous practice of the Steps. Our ability to work Step Ten is based on our understanding of Steps Four through Nine and on how completely we implemented those Steps.

STEP TEN

Continued to take personal inventory and, when we were wrong, promptly admitted it.

Be serious and frequent in the examination of your heart and life . . . Every evening review your carriage through the day—what you have done or thought that was unbecoming your character. Have a special care of two portions of time, namely, morning and evening; the morning to forethink what you have to do, and the evening to examine whether you have done what you ought. —JOHN WESLEY

In Step Ten, we begin the maintenance part of the Steps by combining Steps Four through Nine into an easy-to-use tool to keep us on track. In those earlier Steps, we removed, with God's help, the blockages and blindness that kept us from carrying out our decision in Step Three to turn our will and our lives over to God. Now, with the help of Step Ten, we can ensure that we stay open to the truth about ourselves and others. This continual openness and honesty will allow us unhindered communication with God. This unhindered communication is the subject of Step Eleven.

> *Learning to replace the word* you *with* I *is a gift you can give yourself. It keeps the focus on you and invites healthier conversation. An example of this is "I feel angry when . . ." instead of "You make me angry when . . ." The choice to be angry is always yours.*

One of the benefits of Step Ten is the emotional sobriety it brings. ADD hurts many of us through the brooding and mood swings so common to the disorder. We often feel like balls being bounced from one bumper to the next in a pinball machine. Step Ten is a stabilizing reality check that protects us from the disturbing effects of negative emotions like anger, fear, and resentment. Step Ten helps us quickly face these feelings and deal with deeper issues.

Jason's Story

Dear Spud,
I bet you never thought I'd write. Well, the fact is, I've thought about you a lot since I got out. I wanted to write and tell you that what you told me . . . what you taught me, really works. I mean, I don't think I'll ever be back there. Things are really different now . . . No, I mean *I'm* different now—thanks to you and God.

Before I met you, I was always mad about something. Everybody used to get in my face and piss me off. It was like I couldn't keep from getting mad and then I'd get drunk or loaded or crazy and beat up on someone. Then I'd get arrested. At home I'd say things I shouldn't, and Mom would kick me out. But it's different now. Like I said, *I'm* different.

The twelve-step meetings sure have helped me out in the real world. They're a lot different from the meetings inside—I don't just mean because there's women. These dudes are real people, and I feel kinda special when I go. They make me deal with my resentments and fears just like you used to. In fact, there's one old guy that reminds me of you. When I get into my "old stuff" and start to rag on somebody, he shuts me up. He asks me what part of me feels hurt and why I'm upset. Then he helps me turn it around. He helps me "grow flowers in the shit" like you used to do. When I'm with him, I don't miss you so much. I think I'm gonna ask him to be my sponsor.

Oh, I went to see my old doctor. When I asked him about some medicine for my ADD, he asked me what kind of a nut I was to think he'd give me some Ritalin. His comment was, "I don't prescribe drugs to druggies—especially prison druggies." You can bet how my temper flared—I wanted to deck the idiot and wreck his office. But it wasn't worth my time to tell him what I'd learned about addicts taking Ritalin. I'm gonna ask Bud if he knows a good doc who won't mind seeing somebody with ADD who's an ex-druggie who's done some time.

I'll tell ya, Spud, the outside world is a crazy place. I feel real lonely out here, but with God looking out for me and with people helping me, I think I'll make it. Thanks for all you taught me and did for me, Spud. And thanks for helping me see my good side.

Hell, I *really* know how crazy the world is every time I think about me being out here and somebody as nice as you being in there.

Your friend,
Jason

> When an uncomfortable feeling arises or when emotional pain warns you that something has gone wrong or is about to go wrong, think of a HALO. Handle it, Analyze it, Let it go, and Omit it from your thoughts. This will keep you on top of your behavior, and more able to do God's will.

Step Ten is a shorthand version of Steps Four through Nine, and is worked in much the same way. The difference is the early detection and prompt handling of the problem. We don't let it sit and fester, to the point where it becomes harmful to us and to our relationships. When we detect an uncomfortable feeling it can usually be traced to resentment, fear, or guilt and remorse over something we did. We make note—either mentally or in writing—of who or what is associated with that feeling. Then we ask ourselves what occurred to create the feeling. These points need to be noted, so that we can determine what part of our self was threatened.

When we have identified who or what we resent or fear, the reason for our guilt and remorse, and what happened to cause it, we need to let go of it. We can't do anything to change it. We can only acknowledge that it happened and determine what caused us to react. Our original uncomfortable feeling or behavior was a reaction or an ADD "hyperreaction" to some real or imagined threat. We now identify the area of our life that was threatened, and make note of it. It happened, so we need to let it go and give it to God.

> *I've heard people say "Stuff Happens." That's true. I'm learning that I can't stop bad things from happening in my life, but I can choose how I will respond to them when they do happen. Someone said, "Pain is inevitable, but misery is optional." With the right attitude, a big dose of hope, and God's help, I can face what life brings.*

We *do* have a choice about how we act. We can identify the character defects or objectionable behaviors that threaten to step in and take over. It is important to make note of the defects involved, admit them, and then ask God to remove them. Hopefully, we recognize our shortcomings before they cause us to react against another person and cause harm. But if we need to make amends because harm has already been done, we do it as soon as we can.

In time, we will develop an even shorter version of this inventory method. We will be able to cut straight to the threat, identify the character defect that has come to the surface, and deal with it. This method of naming, analyzing, and letting go becomes a positive way to handle our problems, identify their causes and conditions, and use the Steps to get rid of them. The more we use the Steps the more skilled we will become at using them. Remember that pain is a signal that something has gone wrong or is about to go wrong. When pain appears, it's a warning sign to get busy and do Step Ten.

"Hyperreactivity" is more common among people with ADD than hyperactivity is. Hyperactivity keeps people with ADD moving on the outside; hyperreactivity keeps them moving on the inside. The emotional pot is always bubbling. This is especially troubling when the idea being reacted to is a resentment or a fear. The emotional brew that results can quickly lead to problem behavior.

Step Ten points the way toward continued spiritual growth. In the past, we were constantly burdened by the results of our inattention to what we were doing. We allowed small problems to become large ones by ignoring them until they multiplied. Because we couldn't properly observe ourselves, our ineffective behavior created havoc in our lives. In Step Ten, we consciously examine our daily conduct and admit our wrongs where necessary. We look at ourselves, see our errors, promptly admit them, then seek God's guidance in correcting them.

Step Ten is neither a new process nor something we do only at night before we go to bed. It is Steps Four through Nine done every day as a habit, all during the day. It is a way to maintain balance and serenity by taking inventory of our thoughts, feelings, and actions. There are three types of inventories: spot-check, daily, and long-term periodic. They each have a specific purpose, and are handled in different ways.

The spot-check inventory involves stopping whenever we have an uncomfortable feeling or a sudden change in mood or behavior. We take a few minutes to quickly review Steps Four through Nine. This keeps us in touch with our feelings and behavior, and reminds us to take action quickly when necessary. It also helps us to stay free from resentment, fear, or guilt and remorse over something we did or are about to do.

> *You can use structure to give yourself the sense of balance that is often lacking in adults with ADD. Some suggestions on how to do this are: Take time from work to go for a walk or have lunch with a friend; Give yourself some idle time in the midst of a strenuous project (the work won't go away); Spend your money, but tuck some of it away in a piggy bank or safe hiding place.*

The daily inventory can be taken at the end of each day or at the beginning of the next. It can be viewed as a balance sheet for the day—a summary of good and bad—and an opportunity to reflect on our interaction with others. We can feel good about situations where we handled ourselves appropriately, and acknowledge our progress. In situations where we tried and failed, we can acknowledge ourselves for trying. We can then make amends where necessary and move forward with peace of mind. The more familiar we become with Step Ten, the more quickly we will be able to catch ourselves before we do something we will regret later.

A long-term periodic inventory offers a special opportunity to renew our intention to live healthier and more fulfilling lives. We set aside some time to be alone so we can review our progress, recognize problem areas and patterns, and make the necessary changes. It is a time to acknowledge traits and qualities that we did not identify in Step Four. It can also be a special time to consider how we can get the most from our positive qualities, like our wonderful gift of humor, which has social and physical benefits. To complete the long-term inventory, it is helpful to attend a retreat or simply find a place where we can be alone and quiet—free from the everyday chaos of life. This inventory will help us see the remarkable changes we have made, renew our hope and courage, and remind us that our progress is a product of God's help.

No matter how hard we try, and no matter how committed we are to working the Steps, situations will arise to challenge our stability and commitment. We need to be as honest and clear as possible about what is happening, and promptly take corrective action. We may be tempted to control and manipulate others, lie or make excuses to deny our ADD-related behavior, react to negative tapes, feel inferior, distract ourselves with obsessive or compulsive behavior, or feel depressed, anxious, or worried. When we note such behavior or feelings, we need to acknowledge the problem, determine its cause, share our insights with a supportive friend, make any necessary amends, and turn it over to God's care.

Scripture tells us that "A merry heart doeth good like a medicine." It's true that laughter is healing. Norman Cousins, in his book The Anatomy of an Illness, documents how his fatal condition was reversed by the power of mirth—not medicine. ADD gives you a leg up on others when it comes to humor. Use your gift of humor—it's great therapy for the body, mind, and spirit!

If we sincerely want to change our lifestyle, we take personal inventory regularly and continue to interact with others in recovery. This reminds us that we are not unique—that everyone gets upset occasionally and no one is always "right." Through this awareness, we develop the ability to forgive and love others. By being kind, courteous, and fair, we will often receive the same treatment in return and can expect to achieve harmony in many of our relationships. As we progress in our recovery, we see how pointless it is to become angry or to allow others to inflict emotional pain on us. We'll be less inclined to harbor resentments toward others if we take inventory regularly and promptly admit our wrongs.

> *The quality of my life is up to me. I know that I am responsible for what happens to me. I can't blame anyone else—not even God. When it's someone else's fault, there is nothing I can do about it. When it's my fault, I am free—free to make it right.*

As we daily work the Steps, we develop a discipline, deepen our love for God, become more aware of others, experience genuine sorrow for our wrongs, and improve our relationships. God molds our character as we daily face our faults and promptly correct them. Delay in admitting our wrongs is harmful—it lessens the effectiveness of Step Ten. But if we promptly take a personal inventory, we will see positive results. Our relationship problems will diminish, and misunderstandings will be easier to resolve. We will honestly express ourselves and be less concerned about our need to "pass for normal." We will pay attention to our own wrongs and show respect and consideration for others instead of looking for fault. Our self-esteem will improve, and we will feel good about ourselves and our abilities.

Key Ideas

Personal inventory: The personal inventory in Step Ten is similar to the moral inventory in Step Four. The difference is it's continuous. The word *personal* reminds us that the inventory process is about us, not about others.

Spot-check inventory: The spot-check inventory is done several times during the day as a check against slipping into negative feelings and inappropriate behavior. Throughout the day we note problem situations as they occur and take action to correct them. The helps us to respond in good character and not react to the threat as we did in the past.

Daily inventory: Quality time every day should be set aside for our daily inventory. This can be a few minutes before bed or early in the morning when our minds are clear. It is best to use a personal journal or the inventory log. This inventory will serve as a reminder that progress is being made—one day at a time.

Long-term periodic inventory: The long-term periodic inventory, done every three months, twice a year, or annually, is a thorough inventory that covers an extended period of time. This allows us to see patterns and changes in our lives—good and bad. It is helpful to find some form of retreat or a place of solitude to make this inventory.

 Prayer for Step Ten

I pray I may continue:
To grow in understanding and effectiveness;
To take daily spot-check inventories of myself;
To correct mistakes when I make them;
To take responsibility for my actions;
To be ever aware of my negative and self-defeating attitudes and behaviors;
To keep my willfulness in check;
To always remember I need your help;
To keep love and tolerance of others as my code; and
To continue in daily prayer to ask how I can best serve you,
My Higher Power.

PERSONAL INVENTORY

STEP FOUR			
COLUMN 1	**COLUMN 2**	**COLUMN 3**	**COLUMN 4**
I (resent, fear, harmed)	because	This affects my	My wrongs were
Grace	*she cheated on me*	*emotional security*	*envy and anger*
1			
2			
3			
4			
5			
6			
7			

INSTRUCTIONS FOR COMPLETION

STEP FOUR

Column 1 List the people, institutions, or principles you resent, fear, or harmed.

Column 2 List what happened to cause the resentment, fear, or harm.

Column 3 List your needs or ambitions that were affected: social, security, or sexual.

Column 4 List the nature of your wrongs, faults, defects, or shortcomings that surfaced because of the resentment, fear, or harm.

This worksheet will help you keep a current inventory of the resentments, fears, or harm done to others. It is a shorthand version of Steps Four through Nine, and will enable you to quickly handle situations that arise. The worksheet can be used for the spot-check, daily, and long-term periodic inventories.

STEP FIVE	STEPS SIX AND SEVEN	STEP EIGHT	STEP NINE
COLUMN 5	COLUMN 6	COLUMN 7	COLUMN 8
I will admit it to	I will ask God to remove my shortcomings because	How I harmed the person and myself	How and when I will make amends
My therapist	I don't like how I feel	I told her sister about it	in person, when I see her

STEP FIVE
Column 5 List the person with whom you will share Step Five.
STEPS SIX AND SEVEN
Column 6 List why you will ask God to remove your shortcomings.
STEP EIGHT
Column 7 List how you harmed the person.
STEP NINE
Column 8 List how and when you will make amends.

It's hard to believe how much my life has changed since I began working the Steps. I am using Step Ten to monitor my behavior, and I feel a lot better about myself. Some of the ways that Step Ten has helped me are:

_____

_____

_____

_____

_____

_____

_____

_____

_____

_____

_____

_____

_____

_____

_____

_____

STEP TEN REVIEW

Step Ten points the way toward continued spiritual growth. We examine our daily conduct and make adjustments where necessary. We look at ourselves, see our errors, promptly admit them, and take corrective action. A daily inventory makes us more conscious of our actions, and helps us keep our commitment to change our behavior. We are less inclined to yield to feelings of loneliness, self-righteousness, and anger if we remain emotionally balanced. We become more capable of living our lives in a way that promotes health and a sense of well-being.

❏ List an example that shows you are relating better to others.

❏ Cite a recent situation in which you did not behave appropriately. What did you do when you realized you were in error?

❏ How does taking a daily inventory support your spiritual growth?

❏ Cite an example in which correcting your wrongs saved you from unnecessary consequences.

11

UNDERSTANDING STEP ELEVEN

"Every morning," the former Navy man recalled, "the boatswain's mate would pipe muster, and we all hurried to our appointed places. Once muster was piped, we got the word for the day from our chief. And we'd be reminded to look at the plan of the day for other news. We always knew exactly what to do!"

Step Eleven is our call to muster—to draw near to our Higher Power and get the word and plan for the day. Back in Step Three, we made the decision to turn our will and our lives over to God's care. Next, we had to actually do it. But things like self-will and troublesome ADD behavior blocked us from carrying out that decision. So we jumped into action—Steps Four through Nine. In Step Ten, we started the maintenance part of our journey, doing Steps Four through Nine every day. Step Eleven is "putting into action" our Step Three decision to let God direct our lives.

WORKING STEP ELEVEN

We work Step Eleven by practice of prayer and meditation. Through prayer we talk to God; through meditation we listen to God. Many of us struggle with this because we are unfamiliar with it, or because it is hard for us to sit quietly and concentrate. It is important that we make an effort to do this, because we need the structure, the plan, and the purpose that communication with God provides.

PREPARING FOR STEP ELEVEN

We prepare for Step Eleven by taking prayer and meditation seriously. Many of us have a tendency to put prayer and meditation on the second shelf and treat them as unimportant or unnecessary. If we struggle in this area, we might seek counsel with a therapist, talk with an experienced program member, or seek help from a friend.

STEP ELEVEN

Sought through prayer and meditation to improve our conscious contact with God as we understood God, praying only for knowledge of God's will for us and the power to carry that out.

I have been driven many times to my knees by the overwhelming conviction that I had nowhere else to go. —ABRAHAM LINCOLN

Steps Four through Ten helped us overcome the blockages that kept us from carrying out the decision we made in Step Three—to turn our will and our lives over to the care of God. ADD made us feel like round pegs in square holes, so we took control of our own lives, thinking we could make things fit—that we could pass for normal. We did everything we could to make life work according to our plan. And when things didn't go our way, we looked for ways to kill the pain or to escape. All these manifestations of self-will blinded us and kept us from knowing and doing God's will.

In Step Eleven we carry out the decision to turn our will and our lives over to God's care. As a result of Steps Four

> I just remembered the self-esteem exercise I did in Step Two. What a trip! I can now look at myself in the mirror and say things like "I belong; I am somebody; I can do something; I can do right; I can make it happen." This must be what the Promises are all about!

through Nine, the truth has set us free and removed the blockages that hindered us. We are no longer slaves to the survival skills, character traits, and self-defeating behavior that kept us from doing the good that our Creator had put in our hearts. We are well on the road to changing the direction of our lives. And changing direction is going to change our lives dramatically.

Tracey's Story

 Dear God,
You know it's really hard for me to pray or meditate, because my mind won't stop thinking about a thousand things when I'm trying to be quiet.

Thanks to my ADD diagnosis, the Twelve Steps, and a new kind of relationship with you, I understand myself and others a lot better. When I first realized how ADD had affected my life and others' lives, I wanted to give up on self-improvement. I couldn't believe what others thought of me and how much harm I'd done without even knowing it! I always believed I was doing the right thing—taking care of my family, trying to be the perfect wife, managing the business, and providing for the employees. But behind my back, people called me power-hungry, obsessive, and controlling.

I always thought that the employees respected me. I didn't see myself as demanding, obsessive, or critical. Yes, I have an idea a minute and can change my mind in a flash, but I never dreamed this affected the workers. When I thought they understood and agreed with me, they were worrying about how to implement my latest idea and still get their own work done. I realize now that they weren't honest with me.

Another thing I never grasped was the unrealistic deadlines I placed on others. In my ADD-crazed world, with my unrelenting energy, I believed anything was possible. I could be on the go sixteen hours a day and keep track of ten projects at the same time without feeling tired. Others got tired just thinking about what I did and felt threatened because they couldn't keep up.

I moved so fast that I never really sensed the employees' reaction to me. I never was very good at picking up clues about people's feelings. When I'd ask my secretary how she was, I'd only hear part of her response. I'd wait for the right moment to inter-rupt, so I could ask when she would have the mar-keting plan ready.

Well, God, I know you understand how sorry I am for all the chaos and sadness I've created. If I'd known any different, I'd have been different. I'm more at peace with myself too. Step Eleven is my favorite, because if I run into a brick wall, I can take a deep breath and pray for an intuitive thought on how to resolve my dilemma. To this day, you have never let me down—the answer always comes when I need it.

God, thanks for being there for me—and thanks for understanding how difficult it is for me to sit quietly and pray or meditate.

Much love,
Tracey

Step Eleven provides a structured way to engage in prayer and meditation. For people with ADD, this struc-ture can be very helpful in developing a successful way to pray and meditate. Although prayer and meditation are often difficult because of our ADD-related behavior, they are a vital part of the program.

Learn how to give up. An admirable trait is your never-say-die attitude. How-ever, sometimes it is better to say die. If you have been fired from six sales jobs in a row, ask God for direction before you apply for another one.

They put into action what we decided to do in Step Three when we gave up directing and turned our lives over to God's care. In Step Eleven we receive God's direction and find out from God how to run our lives. Remember: It's not *how* you pray or meditate that is important—but simply that you *do* it.

The discipline of prayer and meditation in Step Eleven requires a lot of work and a deep sense of commitment. It takes the work of the first ten Steps, and then it takes continuous practice over a long period of time. The discipline involves time for evening, morning, and during-the-day prayer and meditation.

Evening Prayer and Meditation

At the end of the day we should pray and meditate as a way to gain perspective on the day just lived. We ask ourselves a number of questions and review our conduct, attitude, and progress during the day. Being as honest as possible will make the results more positive, so it is important to give careful thought to this process. For example:

- Were we resentful, selfish, dishonest, or afraid?
- Were we impatient, disrespectful, or impulsive?
- Were we self-centered and inconsiderate toward others?
- Did we do something for which we must make amends?
- Were we kind, tolerant, and loving?
- Did we think of what we could do for others?
- Did we give something back to life?
- What could we have done better?

> *A lot of books have been written about the practice of prayer and meditation, but very few have put it as simply as Bill W. did in the Big Book of* Alcoholics Anonymous *(pages 86–88). His recommendations included asking spouses or friends to join in on morning meditation, reading books about prayer, attending morning devotions at a church, memorizing a few prayers, or seeking help from a priest, minister, or rabbi.*

When we finish our reflection, we make note of the things we need to work on and ask God to help us do better tomorrow. We reflect on our behavior and ask God's help in determining what corrective measures must be taken. It is important that we don't dwell on our mistakes and drift into worry and shame over our behavior. The idea is to keep improving, not to become stressed and anxious over what we are doing wrong. Once we make the review, discuss it with God, commit ourselves to doing better, and accept God's love and mercy, we can settle down and get a good night's sleep—free from guilt and remorse.

Part of doing God's will means taking action and trusting that my Higher Power is working through me. I remember being told to pray as if it all depends on God, and to work as if it all depends on me.

Morning Prayer and Meditation

Each morning we think about the day ahead. With paper and pen in hand, we list our plans for the day. Because our minds are so full of ideas, details, and urgent impulses, it is important that we write down whatever comes to mind. In that way we can feel assured that nothing will be left out. Our goal is not to produce a to-do list, but to seek God's direction and will throughout the day in all our endeavors.

Based on the program principles and the direction they provide, our attitude toward prayer changes as we work the Steps. We learn to ask that God's will for our lives be shown to us, and we trust that our best interests will be served. The old habit of praying for material things will diminish, to be replaced with prayers for guidance. We begin to rely on some of the slogans and prayers, such as "Let go and let God" or the Serenity Prayer. We trust that God will hear and respond to our most humble call for aid, even if our prayer is as simple as "God, please help me" or "Thank you, Higher Power."

> Because of your tendency to drift off and lose attention quickly, you need structured time if you want to be successful with Step Eleven. To make the process of prayer and meditation easier, consider these helpful hints: make a prayer list; set a time limit; find an appropriate place; and use aids (prayer books, candles, music, etc.).

Prayer and Meditation throughout the Day

During the day we will most likely be faced with moments of frustration, anxiety, indecision, impatience, confusion, or distraction. We can struggle with the problem or we can realize the need for guidance from our Higher Power and turn the problem over. By letting go of the problem we don't solve it, but we free ourselves to focus on other things. We can go on with our lives and forget about *that* problem. When we have given up wrestling with the problem and turned it over to God, the right answer will come. A quick and effective way to bring God into the picture is to say, "Thy will be done," or "God, please send me an intuitive thought." When we get accustomed to calling on God for help, we have more energy because we're not wearing ourselves out trying to arrange our lives to suit ourselves.

Once we stop wrestling with our problems, the answers come. We will find that hunches and inspiration gradually work their way into our minds. The answers will also come from others, for God uses all kinds of people and different ways to speak to us. If we place our will in God's hands and pray sincerely for guidance, we find that our will is being redirected. We then gain the courage and power to

> Many of the AA slogans are very appropriate for adults with ADD. One in particular is "God gave us two ears but only one mouth because God wants us to spend twice as much time listening as talking, and God knows listening is twice as hard as talking."

act according to God's will for us. Seeking higher guidance is an experience in humility, because we are so accustomed to running our lives by our own plan and so used to making demands on God to give us what we think we want or need. Sometimes our own desires and opinions are so much a part of us that we may mistake our own ideas for our Higher Power's will.

If we are progressing satisfactorily with Step Eleven by praying and meditating, we will see signs along the way. We will feel more at peace in our daily affairs, experience deep gratitude for our ongoing healing, and feel as though we have finally achieved our rightful place in the world. Feelings of self-worth will replace feelings of shame. These signs tell us that God is guiding and sustaining our recovery.

> *The physical effects of an angry outburst, common to men with ADD, can last for hours. Try to reduce your anger and frustration through exercise, meditation, and proper sleep. Limit alcohol intake, which alters moods, and seek therapy if necessary.*

When we combine prayer and meditation with self-examination, we discover the secret to successfully working the Steps. We also discover an effective means for maintaining a rewarding spiritual life. No matter how dedicated we are to recovery, we all have moments of doubt about the direction of our lives. We may even question the need to continue working the Steps. Sometimes we are tempted to regress to our old behavior. We tend to be especially vulnerable when we feel pressured for accomplishment or when we expect events to follow our own time schedule. In our frustration, we seize control from God's hands and attempt to hasten the process through our own willfulness. When we do this we are not following God's guidance, and we must renew the commitment we made in Step Three.

 **Key Ideas**

Prayer: Prayer is communication with our Higher Power, and is most effective when it is honest and frequent. It is fitting to complain to God, to thank God, to share the details of our lives with God, to praise God, and to talk to God as we would talk to a trusted friend. Avoid "wish-list" prayers that ask God for something, and remember that our main goal is to seek and know God's will for us, so that we can carry it out.

Meditation: Meditation is listening prayer. We quiet our hearts, minds, and bodies so that our spirits might hear our Higher Power. It is a spiritual exercise that is most effective when we can be quiet and reflective. If this isn't possible, do what works for you, whether it is walking, sitting under a tree, or looking out your window and daydreaming.

Conscious contact: For many years zealous believers of various faiths have used "prayer rocks" to remind themselves to pray. Tiny pebbles in their shoes reminded them with every step to reach out to God. Fist-sized stones under their pillows prompted them to pray even as they retired to sleep. Although we may not agree that we need rocks in our shoes and beds to remind us to pray, we should agree that constant contact with our Higher Power is necessary.

God's will: Before any building, highway, or development is physically constructed, an architect develops a detailed plan for the project. With the architect's plans and blueprints, the builders and workers can do the work required. In a similar sense, we realize that our Higher Power is the preferred architect for our own lives. God's will for our lives is the plan we desire to follow. We use prayer and meditation to get God's blueprint for each new day as it comes.

Prayer for Step Eleven

Higher Power,
You know my needs before I ask
My heart before I pray,
And my gratitude
Before I even offer my thanks.
You understand me better
Than I understand myself,
And I thank you for communicating with me
In the language of the heart.

SERENITY PRAYER EXERCISE

God, grant me the serenity	This exercise will show you how to use the Serenity Prayer as a way of processing and accepting situations that trouble you.	
To accept the things I cannot change	the courage to change the things I can	and the wisdom to know the difference
how I was treated as a child	to get rid of my negative tapes	between what I can and can't change

---

Serenity Prayer

God, grant me the serenity
To accept the things I cannot change,
The courage to change the things I can,
And the wisdom to know the difference.

Reinhold Niebuhr

STEP ELEVEN REVIEW

To protect what we have gained, we must continually seek to know our Higher Power's will for us. To discover this will, we must establish communication through a daily regimen of prayer and meditation. Our approach to **Step Eleven** will vary in intent and intensity. Prayer can take many forms, ranging from a simple cry for help to an extended review at the end of the day. Meditation may seem impossible if we think it requires emptying our busy ADD minds. But when we realize that a thoughtful nature walk or the careful consideration of a spiritual writing are also forms of meditation, we reap rich rewards.

❏ Cite an example in which your Higher Power answered your prayers through another person or a new experience.

❏ Describe a situation in which you delayed taking action because you were "waiting" for God's will. What happened?

❏ What difficulties do you have in prayer and meditation? How can you overcome them?

❏ Describe your current relationship with your Higher Power.

12

UNDERSTANDING STEP TWELVE

Most houses with children have a wall or a doorpost with pencil marks. These keep track of growth. Every few months the kids back up against the wall for Mom or Dad to mark their height. Sometimes the growth is barely noticeable, sometimes quite dramatic.

Step Twelve is a time for measuring growth. We realize that the spiritual part of ourselves has been awakened. Through God's goodness and our commitment to working the Steps, a new king sits on the throne—God. With God's help, we've given up our crown and put God in charge of our kingdom. Although we have grown a lot through this process, the mark on the wall isn't as high as it used to be—we've taken off our crown.

WORKING STEP TWELVE

Step Twelve involves taking time to appreciate the spiritual growth in our lives. We work this Step by sharing the program with others and continuing to practice the principles of the Twelve Steps in all our affairs. It is especially important that we take time to help newcomers and to share our story with them.

PREPARING FOR STEP TWELVE

We prepare for Step Twelve by going through the other eleven Steps and reaching a point where we are ready to share our stories with others. Because we have seen the program work for us, we can reach out to others and help them come to believe. Our spiritual awakening is a result of working the Steps, and to keep it we must continue to work them. Carrying the message to others and practicing the principles in all our affairs are important keys to being able to keep what we have received.

STEP TWELVE

Having had a spiritual awakening as the result of these Steps, we tried to carry this message to others, and to practice these principles in all our affairs.

Amazing grace! How sweet the sound that saved a wretch like me! I once was lost, but now am found, was blind, but now I see. —JOHN NEWTON

In Step Twelve we celebrate the joy of living and demonstrate that joy through action. This joy is a product of a spiritual awakening that, for many of us, came gradually as we worked the Steps. This spiritual awakening enables us to think, believe, and feel things in ways we couldn't do before, and allows us to call up our own strength and resources. We have been granted a gift that amounts to a new state of consciousness and being. We know we are on the right road—that we have turned away from a dead-end street. We can now appreciate that life is something to be enjoyed rather than endured.

In a sense, we have been transformed. We have tapped an inner resource of strength

 Continue to learn what you can about ADD, so that you can help others find relief. Sharing your experience, strength, hope, and some facts about ADD can have a powerful influence on helping others find ways to live happier and healthier lives.

that we didn't know we had. Our spirit is awakened and we find ourselves possessing degrees of honesty, tolerance, peace of mind, and love that we thought were beyond our reach. What we have received is a gift—one that we have worked hard to earn and have prepared ourselves to receive.

Charlene's Story

 "Our next speaker," the conference leader said, "is here to talk about ADD from a spiritual perspective. Please welcome Charlene."

"Hi, I'm Charlene. I'm here today because I want to share with you how the Twelve Steps are helping me to live with ADD. It wasn't until I was diagnosed with ADD that I was able to fully understand my behavior and the problems I continually encountered, regardless of how committed I was to my program. Although my relationship with my Higher Power was improving, my mood swings and anxiety were always there, no matter what I did. My story isn't unique, but being here and carrying the message of the Twelve Steps is something that helps me to keep what I have by giving it away.

"I am a recovering prescription-drug addict. I used to spend my days trying to numb, cover up, or kill any hint of pain or discomfort I felt. I used tranquilizers, painkillers, muscle relaxers, sleeping pills, and alcohol in my attempt to accomplish this.

"During my 'using' days, I was a youth counselor at my church, preaching about living what I thought to be a good life. But because I was using drugs at the time, my relationship with God was only skin deep, and I received little benefit from God's presence. I knew God, and I preached to the group about the importance of God in their lives, but I didn't include God in my own heart or in my life.

"Things changed when I met Briana. She was a recovering alcoholic who wanted to give something back. I noticed right away that she had peace, confidence, stability, inner strength, and more. She had what I preached to the kids about, but didn't possess myself. I'm ashamed to say it, but I wanted her gone. I felt uncomfortable taking my pills when she was there—like I was lying to my students.

"I realize now that God was speaking to me through Briana. It was through Briana's sharing her story that I found the Twelve Steps and a new relationship with my Higher Power. I started attending meetings, gave up drugs, and began to change my life. It wasn't easy, but it has become the greatest gift I ever gave myself.

"Through a renewed relationship with my Higher Power and a willingness to change, I have been able to enjoy many of the things I saw in Briana. I am experiencing peace, am doing better in my relationships, and am feeling really good about myself. Since my ADD diagnosis, I've seen how much the Steps can help me in changing my behavior to cope with my ADD tendencies. I have to believe I will feel *really* good when some of my ADD-related behavior changes.

"For me, the Twelve Steps really work. When I see myself getting distracted, I recite Step Two; if I get angry, I take a few deep breaths and work Step Ten. I have found a 'prescription' drug that works for me—that treats my *real* problem.

"I'm free today. Free to feel, free to trust, free to be who I am, free to let others be themselves. I don't have to control my world. I've found someone bigger, stronger, and wiser who already has things under control. I gave God my life, and God gave it back more abundantly than I ever could have dreamed."

Carrying the message to others and sharing your own experience is a safeguard against losing what you have gained. An old-timer summarized this process in one short sentence when he said, "To keep it you have to give it away."

In Step Twelve we carry the message of hope and healing to others. Our responsibility is only to carry the message—what people do with it is not our concern. Many of us were introduced to this program by someone who was working Step Twelve by carrying the message to us. Now we have the opportunity to enhance our own growth by giving away what was so freely given to us. When we talk to a newcomer, we don't talk about anything we "believe." We talk instead about what we know through personal experience and about the principles that brought results in our lives. This program calls us to live our principles daily and share with others the healing power of the Steps.

When we make a habit of giving away what we have received, our lives will take on new meaning. We will be able to watch people recover, see them help others, and watch our circle of friends grow. If we kept the gift of the Steps to ourselves, we would miss these pleasures. Frequent contact with newcomers and others in the program is a bright spot in our lives, and keeps us ever mindful that our symptoms won't disappear—they will merely become more manageable.

This Step reminds us that our twelve-step work is never done. When daily challenges distract and separate us from our Higher Power, we can use the Steps as tools to face our problems and return to God's will. Step One reminds us that we are powerless to help ourselves through self-will alone. Step Two lifts our eyes to a Power greater than ourselves. Step Three brings us to the only sane decision—to choose God's will and direction. Step Four requires self-examination. Step Five moves us from isolation as we share our self-discoveries with another. Step Six prepares us to say goodbye to the defects of character we have lived with for so long. Step Seven guides us through humble prayer for the removal of our shortcomings. Step Eight continues our housekeeping when we list the people we harm. Step Nine takes us through the process of making amends as we repair the damage we do. Step Ten continues the self-examination and process of making amends every day. Step Eleven keeps us in contact with our Higher Power as a source of guidance and inspiration.

"Actions speak louder than words" is an accurate description of how we should carry the twelve-step message to others. People act much more positively when they see a principle being applied than when they just hear a lecture about theory. Our willingness to acknowledge our shortcomings, make amends, release our resentments and fears, and

Great job! You've made it to Step Twelve and come out a winner. Don't forget the importance of daily practice—it keeps you in shape and in touch with other teammates. And most important: spend time coaching the rookies!

trust God will demonstrate the power of the Twelve Steps. By sharing our personal story, we offer people a way to tap their own inner resources and resolve their problems. Through our story we can convey a message of strength and hope to others who are looking for new strength and direction in their lives.

Working with newcomers is rewarding and exciting. Many of them are troubled, confused, and resentful—like we once were. They need guidance and help to understand that God can strengthen and change them. Our job is to encourage them to seek the rewards and miracles that are possible through the Steps. Our most effective tool is sharing our own experience, strength, and hope. If we talk only about principles, others may have trouble connecting those principles to everyday life. But when we tell our story, it is real. When we share our own experience we invite newcomers to find themselves in our story.

Sharing our story can be a growth experience for us as well as an opportunity for someone to follow our path. By reflecting on ourselves when we were first introduced to the

> When planning to share your story, take some time to prepare what you want to say. Acknowledge your need for structure and your tendency to think too fast. Write an outline (it can be as short as a few key words) or write a prepared speech to deliver at a twelve-step meeting. A simple format could be: life before the program, how you were introduced to the Steps, and how they work for you. Share your own recovery as a way to offer encouragement.

program, we can see how far we have come, how far we have risen on the growth scale. When carrying the message to someone who is just starting the journey, we can offer our understanding by saying, "I've been there, and I understand how you feel. I made my decision after I had suffered enough, was discouraged enough, and had hit bottom."

At times we may become discouraged and lose sight of our progress. If this happens, we can take a few minutes to review the Milestones in Recovery and measure our progress. Like children who gaze at the marks on the wall to see how much they have grown, we can see our own growth. We have worked very hard to reach these milestones, and now we can rejoice in how much we have achieved.

Newcomers may or may not be using medication as part of their treatment. Don't play doctor when it comes to a discussion of medicine, and in no case should you share your medication with another person "just to give it a try." Instead, encourage the person to talk with his or her doctor.

The milestones in recovery are:

■ We are using our resentments, fears, and worries as a means for understanding ourselves, instead of blaming others for our shortcomings.

■ We are enjoying peace and serenity, trusting that God is guiding our recovery.

■ We are gaining a healthy sense of self-esteem and accepting responsibility for our own thoughts, feelings, and actions.

■ We are feeling comfortable with our impulsive nature and learning to use it in positive ways.

■ We are structuring our lives to combat scattered thinking and disorganization.

■ We are accepting distractibility as part of who we are, and scheduling extra time in our day to allow for distractions.

■ We are no longer fearful of others and have stopped isolating ourselves as a way to feel safe and escape from others.

■ We are learning to laugh about our forgetfulness and are finding clues to help us remember where we put things and where we are going.

■ We are becoming more patient and recognizing that God's timing is always right.

■ We are no longer bucking the system; we are learning that we can accomplish more through cooperation than we can through resistance.

■ We are taking on fewer responsibilities and trying to reduce the number of projects we have going simultaneously.

■ We are using our sense of humor to feel more comfortable in social settings.

An important achievement in working the Steps comes when we make them an integral part of our day. The Steps

> *If people had told me six months ago that I could improve my sense of self-esteem by working the Twelve Steps, I would have laughed at them. But as I look at myself now, I see a new and confident person emerging. When I read the Milestones in Recovery and realize how many of them I am experiencing, I can't help but say, "Wow! Look at me!"*

> My progress in recovery gives me a feeling of success. I'm beginning to understand who I am and what I was born to do. I am now free to fashion a lifestyle that enables me to become what God wants me to be. I'm free from the expectations of others and no longer feel like a square peg in a round hole. I'm a me-shaped creation made to fit in a me-shaped hole—designed especially by God.

become second nature as we regularly work out problems and concerns through the twelve-step process. This habit keeps us humble and helps us acknowledge our need for God's guidance. The result is sustained peace and serenity and a new confidence that we can deal directly and effectively with problems and concerns as they arise. Any action we take is then guided by God's will and our honest appraisal of the consequences. We can act confidently and without fear.

At this stage, we can see ourselves as pens through which the ink of our Higher Power flows to write the story of our lives. Our sponsor, those who encouraged our work with the Steps, and the group with whom we used this book have contributed to our deeper contact with God. Sharing each other's experience, strength, and hope has enabled us to expand our faith in our Higher Power and experience unconditional love.

Key Ideas

Spiritual awakening: Step Twelve gives us a guarantee—a promise that our spirit has been awakened by the first eleven Steps. We have identified an inner resource that gives us strength and inspiration to continue on our spiritual path of recovery. We have developed a trust and dependence on God that brings us peace and serenity. We come to Step Twelve with confidence that God can be trusted, that miracles can and do happen, and that prayer works.

Carrying the message: In Step Twelve we carry the message to others whose situations are similar to ours. From *Alcoholics Anonymous* (the Big Book), we realize that early program members understood that they were carrying a spiritual message. The message we carry is that God can redeem us from our shortcomings, our self-defeating behavior, and our despair. We carry a spiritual message that only God is able to control our lives and heal us—that we will live more productive lives if we yield to a Power greater than ourselves.

 Prayer for Step Twelve

Thank you, God,
For all you have given me.
Thank you for all
You have taken from me.
But, most of all,
I thank you, God, for what you've left me:
Recovery, along with peace of mind,
Faith, hope, and love.

WORKING THE STEPS

This exercise will show you how to use the Twelve Steps to deal with a situation in your life that bothers you. Identify a troubling situation or condition that involves a relationship (family, work, or sexual), your work environment, your health, or your self-esteem. Write a brief statement describing the situation. Identify your concern, and then "work the Steps."

Situation:		
Step One	In this situation I am powerless over	
Step Two	I believe my Higher Power can	
Step Three	My decision to turn it over to God is	
Step Four	My shortcomings in this situation are	
Step Five	I will admit the exact nature of my wrongs to	
Step Six	I am willing to release these wrongs because	
Step Seven	My request to have God remove my shortcomings is	
Step Eight	I harmed	
Step Nine	I will make amends by	
Step Ten	Since beginning this exercise I see new issues, such as	
Step Eleven	In my prayer and meditation God showed me	
Step Twelve	My spiritual awakening came as an understanding of	

STEP TWELVE REVIEW

Each of the Twelve Steps is a vital part of fulfilling our Higher Power's plan for us. By conscientious attention to working the Steps, we develop a level of love, acceptance, honesty, and peace of mind we have never known before. **Step Twelve** invites us to promote our own growth by helping others. Our willingness to share our story with others, and our growing awareness of our Higher Power's presence in our lives allow us to give away what we have received.

❑ How has your life improved as a result of working the Steps?

❑ List a concern or problem you had and describe your experience of resolving it by applying the Twelve Steps.

❑ What is your favorite way of "carrying the message" to others in recovery?

❑ Cite an example of telling your story and having someone identify with it. How did you feel?

APPENDIX ONE

THE FACILITATOR'S ROLE

Significant value can be gained if a recovering person who is familiar with this material acts as group facilitator. The facilitator provides support, direction, and encouragement to the participants, and serves as a resource by answering questions relative to the material. This program is not a group therapy situation in which professional advice is given; it is instead an arena in which individuals can share their own experience, strength, and hope.

Even though one person initiates the workshop and may serve as a facilitator, it is important to choose a different meeting leader each week. This gives others an opportunity to gain experience in following the format and conducting the meeting. Recommended formats for the introductory and regular meetings can be found in this appendix. They are provided as a suggestion only, and can be customized to meet each group's specific needs.

Previous Step Studies have revealed that sharing is more effective when done in small groups containing no more than six people. So if twenty-four people attend the meeting, divide them into four groups of six each. The small groups gather to discuss the material and to share with each other for a portion of the meeting. Keeping the groups small allows more time for each person to share. The final portion of the meeting is devoted to sharing in one large group.

The length of time required to complete *The Twelve Steps— A Guide for Adults with Attention Deficit Disorder* varies according to the needs of the group. Before beginning work on the Steps, it is helpful to spend two to three weeks on the material in the front of the book. The first week can include an overview of the introductory materials, the Twelve Steps, and the value of support and fellowship. The second and sometimes the third week can be devoted to reviewing the common symptoms, common traits, and positive qualities. We suggest that one to two weeks be spent on each Step. An additional week may be devoted to the Step review or to the exercises in some of the Steps.

GUIDELINES FOR GROUP PARTICIPANTS

Recognize that your Higher Power is in charge.
▦ Gratefully acknowledge the presence of your Higher Power and pray for guidance and direction.

Make a point of offering love in an appropriate manner.
▦ Respect the needs of others by asking permission to express concern with a hug or a touch. Many people are uncomfortable with physical contact.

Focus individual sharing on the step, exercise, or topic being covered.
▦ Focus sharing on individual experience, strength, and hope as it relates to the material being discussed.
▦ Allow equal time for everyone in the group to share.

Limit talking and allow others to share.
▦ Keep your comments brief; take turns talking; and don't interrupt others.
▦ Respect each person's right to self-expression without comment.

Encourage comfort and support by sharing from your own experience.
▦ Do not attempt to give advice or rescue the person who is sharing.
▦ Accept what others say without comment, realizing it is true for them. Assume responsibility only for your own feelings, thoughts, and actions.

Refrain from cross-talk.
▦ Cross-talk occurs when two or more people engage in dialogue that excludes others. It discourages others from participating.

Maintain confidentiality.
▦ Keep whatever is shared in the group confidential to ensure an atmosphere of safety and openness.

Avoid gossip.
▦ Share your own needs and refrain from talking about a person who is absent.

Refrain from criticizing or defending others.
▦ Lovingly hold others accountable for their behavior only if they ask you to do so.
▦ Recognize that you are accountable to your Higher Power, and it is not your place to defend or criticize others.

Come to each meeting prepared and with a supportive attitude.
▦ Before each meeting, read the designated materials and complete any written exercises.
▦ Ask your Higher Power for guidance and a willingness to share openly and honestly each time you communicate with at least one other group participant.

MEETING ANNOUNCEMENT

The Twelve Steps—
A Guide for Adults with ADD

(Organization)

is starting a Step Study for adults with ADD using the Twelve Steps as a model for recovery.

Beginning date: _____

Day: _____ Time: _____

Meeting location: _____

Contact person: _____ Phone: _____

The Twelve Steps—A Guide for Adults with ADD is a book to help adults with ADD to remove unwanted traits and behaviors and to discover the positive traits and gifts that God gave them. This Step Study will focus on how the spiritual principles of the Twelve Steps can help heal damaged emotions, increase mood stability, and improve self-esteem.

This workshop

▓ Provides a support-group environment for sharing with others

▓ Offers a structured approach to working the Twelve Steps

▓ Provides a workable formula for looking at ADD and its related behavior

▓ Is a model for surrendering one's life to a Higher Power

▓ Helps participants identify what interferes with work and personal relationships

▓ Establishes a basis for building on the positive qualities that are common in adults with ADD

MEETING FORMAT FOR WEEK #1

Note to facilitator: Have copies of *The Twelve Steps—A Guide for Adults with ADD* available for purchase.

Welcome: "Welcome to *The Twelve Steps—A Guide for Adults with ADD* Step Study. My name is _____. I am an adult with ADD, and I am your leader for tonight. I will be leading the introductory meetings and the Step One meeting only. When we begin working on the Steps, I will ask for a volunteer to lead the meeting each week."

Prayer: "Please join me for a moment of silence, after which we will recite the (Serenity Prayer or ADD Prayer for Peace)."

Readings: "I have asked _____ to read the Common Symptoms."

"I have asked _____ to read the Common Traits."

Introductions: "Let's take time to go around the room and introduce ourselves by first name only. Explain briefly why you are here and what you hope to achieve by participating in this Step Study. I'll start."

Program introduction: "Tonight we will be reading and then discussing the introductory material, the Twelve Steps as they apply to adults with ADD, and the importance of support and fellowship as part of the recovery process."

"I will begin by reading 'About This Book' and 'About Using This Book' and will ask for volunteers to participate with me. Please turn to page 4. After the reading is complete I will answer questions."

"We will now begin reading 'About The Twelve Steps' on page 18. I ask that the person on my left read Step One and the next person read the corresponding paragraph. We will rotate around the room until all the Steps have been read."

General sharing: "The meeting is now open for 25 minutes of general sharing. I will begin by sharing my experience of working the Twelve Steps, after which I will ask for volunteers to share their experience."

Support and fellowship: "Please turn to page 26, and I will read 'About Support and Fellowship.' After reading the material, I will answer questions."

Contributions: "Our tradition is to be self-supporting through our own contributions. We ask for your contribution at this time."

Conclusion: "I have asked _____ to read the Promises."

"As we discussed, an important part of the recovery process is working with a sponsor or recovery partner. If anyone here tonight needs help in finding a sponsor or recovery partner, please see me after the meeting. If there is anyone here who would like to volunteer to be a sponsor or recovery partner, please also see me at the end of the meeting."

"You are encouraged to attend other twelve-step meetings as part of your journey."

"Next week we will review the Common Symptoms, Common Traits, and Positive Qualities. If you have a copy of the book, please read the material on pages 29–39. Depending on how much we cover next week, we will either begin Step One, or complete the material on the Common Symptoms, Common Traits, and Positive Qualities."

Closing: "Reminder! Who you see here, what you hear here, stays here. It is not for public disclosure or gossip."

"Please join me in the closing prayer." (Serenity Prayer, ADD Prayer for Peace, The Lord's Prayer, or Prayer of Saint Francis of Assisi)

Note: The suggested time allocation for the meeting is two hours, divided as follows:

Welcome, prayer, and readings:	10 minutes
Introductions:	5 minutes
Program introduction:	45 minutes
General sharing:	25 minutes
Support and fellowship:	15 minutes
Contributions and conclusion:	15 minutes
Closing:	5 minutes

MEETING FORMAT FOR WEEK #2

Note to facilitator: Have copies of *The Twelve Steps—A Guide for Adults with ADD* available for purchase.

Welcome: "Welcome to *The Twelve Steps—A Guide for Adults with ADD* Step Study. My name is _____. I am an adult with ADD, and I am your leader for tonight. I will be leading the introductory meetings and the Step One meeting only. When we begin working on the Steps, I will ask for a volunteer to lead the meeting each week."

Prayer: "Please join me for a moment of silence, after which we will recite the (Serenity Prayer or ADD Prayer for Peace)."

Readings: "I have asked _____ to read the Common Symptoms"

"I have asked _____ to read the Common Traits."

"I have asked _____ to read the Positive Qualities."

"I have asked _____ to read the Twelve Steps."

"I have asked _____ to read the Guidelines for Group Participation."

Introductions: "Let's take time to go around the room and introduce ourselves by first name only. If you were not here last week, explain briefly why you are here and what you hope to achieve by participating in this Step Study. I'll start."

Contributions: "Our tradition is to be self-supporting through our own contributions. We ask for your contribution at this time."

Preparation: "Tonight we will be discussing the Common Symptoms, Common Traits, and Positive Qualities. The material we will be covering begins on page 29. At this time we will break up into small groups of ___ people each. To determine your group, count off by number, then join the group that matches your number."

Small group sharing: "When you are seated, select a person to be the timekeeper, and establish a time limit for sharing based on the number of people in the group. You will have 45 minutes to read and discuss the material. Please spend the next few minutes silently reviewing the material. Choose up to four characteristics about which you would like to share. After the small groups have finished, we will form into a large group and discuss your experiences in the small groups. Sharing is most valuable when you focus on your own personal experience, using 'I' statements."

"Cross-talk is discouraged. Cross-talk occurs when two people have a dialogue that excludes other group members. I'll give a three-minute warning before it is time to rejoin the large group. Please remember to introduce yourself by your first name before you begin sharing."

Large group sharing: "The meeting is now open for general sharing. I will begin by sharing my experience of being in the small group and sharing with others. I will then ask for volunteers to share their experience."

Conclusion: "I have asked _____ to read the Promises."

"An important part of the recovery process is working with a sponsor or recovery partner. If anyone here tonight needs help in finding a sponsor or recovery partner, please see me after the meeting. If there is anyone here who would like to volunteer to be a sponsor or recovery partner, please also see me at the end of the meeting."

"Maintain contact during the week with your sponsor, recovery partner, or someone who is supportive of what you are doing. An alternative to meeting in person is talking on the telephone. You are encouraged to attend other twelve-step meetings as part of your journey."

"Next week we will either complete tonight's materials or begin Step One. I invite input from the group regarding what we will do next week."

Closing: "Reminder! Who you see here, what you hear here, stays here. It is not for public disclosure or gossip."

"Please join me in the closing prayer." (Serenity Prayer, ADD Prayer for Peace, The Lord's Prayer, or Prayer of Saint Francis of Assisi)

Note: The suggested time allocation for the meeting is two hours, divided as follows:

Welcome, prayer, and readings:	10 minutes
Contributions and preparation:	10 minutes
Small group sharing:	45 minutes
Large group sharing:	40 minutes
Conclusion:	10 minutes
Closing:	5 minutes

Regular Meeting Format

Welcome: "Welcome to *The Twelve Steps—A Guide for Adults with ADD* Step Study. My name is _____. I am an adult with ADD, and I am your leader for tonight."

Prayer: "Please join me for a moment of silence, after which we will recite the (Serenity Prayer or ADD Prayer for Peace)."

Readings: "I have asked _____ to read the (Common Symptoms or Common Traits)."

"I have asked _____ to read The Twelve Steps."

"I have asked _____ to read The Twelve Traditions." (First meeting of month)

"I have asked _____ to read the Guidelines for Group Participation."

Contributions: "Our tradition is to be self-supporting through our own contributions. We ask for your contribution at this time."

Introductions and preparation: "Let's take time to go around the room and introduce ourselves by first name only. If you are here for the first time, explain briefly why you are here and what you hope to achieve by participating in this Step Study."

"Tonight we will be discussing Step ____ starting on page ____. At this time we will break up into small groups of ____ people each. To determine your group, count off by number, then join the group that matches your number."

Small group sharing: "When you are seated, select a person to be the timekeeper and establish a time limit for sharing, based on the number of people in your group. You will have 45 minutes to read and discuss the material. Cross-talk is discouraged. Cross-talk occurs when two people have a dialogue that excludes other group members. Sharing is most valuable when you focus on your own personal experience, using 'I' statements. I'll give a three-minute warning before it is time to rejoin the large group. Remember to introduce yourself by your first name before sharing."

Large group sharing: "The meeting is now open for general sharing. If anyone has a positive experience to share, please do so at this time. It is always helpful to hear stories of progress and success. When sharing, include ways in which the Steps helped you to function more effectively. Please raise your hand before sharing."

Conclusion: "I have asked _____ to read (Milestones in Recovery, the Promises, or Positive Qualities)."

"Are there any announcements?"

"Next week we will be discussing Step ____. May I have a volunteer to lead next week's meeting?"

"Maintain contact during the week with your sponsor, recovery partner, or someone who is supportive of what you are doing. An alternative to meeting in person is talking on the telephone. You are encouraged to attend other twelve-step meetings as part of your journey."

"An important part of the recovery process is working with a sponsor or recovery partner. If anyone here tonight needs help in finding a sponsor or recovery partner, please see me after the meeting. If there is anyone here who would like to volunteer to be a sponsor or recovery partner, please also see me at the end of the meeting."

"If we sincerely want to change our lifestyle, we use the Steps daily and continue to interact with others in recovery. Interaction with others reminds us that we are not unique—that everyone gets upset occasionally and no one is always 'right.' Through this awareness, we develop the ability to forgive, understand, and love others for who they are and where they are in their lives. We will grow to see how pointless it is to become angry, allow others to inflict emotional pain on us, and harbor resentments. If we stay committed to working the Steps and staying in contact with others, we will gain a sense of dignity and respect for ourselves and others."

Closing: "Reminder! Who you see here, what you hear here, stays here. It is not for public disclosure or gossip."

"Please join me in the closing prayer." (Serenity Prayer, ADD Prayer for Peace, The Lord's Prayer, or Prayer of Saint Francis of Assisi)

Note: The suggested time allocation for the meeting is two hours, divided as follows:

Welcome, prayer, and readings:	10 minutes
Contributions, introductions, and preparation:	10 minutes
Small group sharing:	45 minutes
Large group sharing:	40 minutes
Conclusion:	10 minutes
Closing:	5 minutes

APPENDIX TWO

SUGGESTED READING LIST

ADD / Self-help

Fowler, Rick and Jerilyn. *Honey, Are You Listening?* Nashville, TN: Thomas Nelson Inc., 1995.

Hallowell, Ed, and Ratey, John. *Driven to Distraction.* New York: Simon & Shuster, 1994.

Hallowell, Ed, and Ratey, John. *Answers to Distraction.* New York: Pantheon Books, 1994.

Hartmann, Thom, *Attention Deficit Disorder: A Different Perception.* Novato, CA: Underwood-Miller, 1993.

Hartmann, Thom. *Focus Your Energy.* New York: Pocket Books, 1994.

Kelly, Kate, and Ramundo, Peggy. *You Mean I'm Not Lazy, Stupid or Crazy?* New York: Scribner, 1993.

Miller, David, and Blum, Kenneth. *Overload—Attention Deficit Disorder and the Addictive Brain*, Kansas City, MO: Andrews and McMeel, 1996.

Solden, Sari. *Women with Attention Deficit Disorder.* Grass Valley, CA: Underwood Books, 1995.

Warren, Paul, and Capehart, Jody. *You and Your ADD Child.* Nashville, TN: Thomas Nelson, 1995.

Weiss, Lynn. *Attention Deficit Disorder in Adults.* Dallas, TX: Taylor Publishing Company, 1992.

Recovery / Self-help

Beattie, Melody. *Codependent No More.* New York: Harper Collins, 1987.

Black, Claudia. *It Will Never Happen to Me.* New York: Ballantine Books, 1987.

Bradshaw, John. *Bradshaw On: The Family.* Deerfield Beach, FL: Health Communications, Inc., 1988.

Brice, Carleen. *Walk Tall—Affirmations for People of Color.* San Diego, CA: RPI Publishing, Inc., 1994.

Friel, John and Linda. *Adult Children—The Secrets of Dysfunctional Families.* Deerfield Beach, FL: Health Communications, Inc., 1987.

Wegscheider-Cruse, Sharon. *Learning to Love Yourself.* Deerfield Beach, FL: Health Communications, Inc., 1987.

Whitfield, Charles. *Healing the Child Within.* Deerfield Beach, FL: Health Communications, Inc., 1989.

Woititz, Janet. *Adult Children of Alcoholics.* Deerfield Beach, FL: Health Communications, Inc., 1990.

Woititz, Janet. *The Intimacy Struggle.* Deerfield Beach, FL: Health Communications, Inc., 1990.

Twelve-step recovery

Alcoholics Anonymous. 3rd edition, New York: Alcoholics Anonymous World Services, Inc., 1976 (The Big Book).

Twelve Steps—Twelve Traditions. New York: Alcoholics Anonymous World Services, Inc., 1981 (The Twelve and Twelve).

Dixon, Angie. *The 12 Steps: An Approach to ADD.* Little Rock, AR: dixon@tce.snider.net

Friends in Recovery. *The 12 Steps for Adult Children.* San Diego, CA: RPI Publishing, Inc., 1996.

Friends in Recovery. *The Twelve Steps—A Spiritual Journey.* San Diego, CA: RPI Publishing, Inc., 1994.

Friends in Recovery. *The Twelve Steps for Christians.* San Diego, CA: RPI Publishing, Inc., 1994.

Friends in Recovery. *The 12 Steps—A Way Out.* San Diego, CA: RPI Publishing, Inc., 1994.

Friends in Recovery. *12 Step Prayers for A Way Out.* San Diego, CA: RPI Publishing, Inc., 1994.

McQ, Joe. *The Steps We Took.* Little Rock, AR: August House Publishers, Inc., 1990.

WHERE TO FIND HELP

The following are programs, organizations, or people from whom you may get more information about ADD or addiction recovery.

ADD information

Attention Deficit Disorder Association (ADDA)
P.O. Box 972
Mentor, OH 44061
(800) 487-2282

> ADDA provides educational resources about attention disorders to individuals and support organizations.

Adult Attention Deficit Foundation
132 North Woodward Avenue
Birmingham, MI 48009
(810) 540-6335

> AADF provides extensive resources and the Copeland test instrument.

CH.A.D.D. National State Networking Committee
(Children and Adults with Attention Deficit Disorder)
499 NW 70th Avenue, Suite 308
Plantation, FL 33317
(305) 587-3700

> CH.A.D.D. is the national and international nonprofit parent-support organization for children and adults with ADD.

Coaching for adults with ADD

Life Coach
124 Waterman St.
Providence, RI 02906
(800) 253-4965; (508) 252-4965
Web: http://www.iquest.net/greatconnectcom/lifecoach

Life Coach is an agency that provides coaches for everyday life. Using the technique developed by Dr. Edward Hallowell, a coach checks in with you by telephone each day and helps you define your objectives for the day. You then make concrete plans to reach your goals as your coach offers you encouragement and positive support.

Coach University
1971 West Lumsden Road, Suite 331
Brandon, FL 33511
(800) 48COACH
Web: htttp://www.coachu.com

Coach University is
■ A company that specializes in training professional coaches
■ A community center for coaches
■ A research and development department for progressive thinking and programs

Coach University offers
■ The Coach University program
■ Coach referral service

The National Coaching Network
Box 253
Lafayette Hill, PA 1944
Telephone and fax (610) 825-4505
Susan Sussman, M. Ed.
(e-mail: 75471.3101@compuserve.com)
Nancy Ratey,. Ed.M. (e-mail: 74472.62@compuserve.com)

The National Coaching Network (NCN) is a national organization dedicated to heightening awareness of ADD coaching and to meeting the needs of people interested in ADD coaching as well as those of people wanting to be coached. NCN provides networking opportunities and educational resources.

TWELVE-STEP SUPPORT GROUPS

Internet Directory of Self-Help Group State Clearinghouses
http://www.tfs.net/personal/iugm/nacr/selfhelp.htm

Internet Directory of Twelve-Step Support Groups
http://www.tfs.net/personal/iugm/nacr/secular.htm

ADD Anonymous
P.O. Box 1193
Julian, CA 92036
(619) 765-2355
e-mail: 74172.1220
@Compuserve.com
Internet Page:
http://users.aol.com/addanon

Adult Children of Alcoholics
Central Service Board
P.O. Box 3216
Torrance, CA 90510
(310) 534-1815

Al-Anon/Alateen
Family Group Headquarters, Inc.
P.O. Box 862
Midtown Station
New York, NY 10018-6106
(212) 302-7240

Alcoholics Anonymous
World Services, Inc.
P.O. Box 475
Riverside Dr., 11th floor
New York, NY 10016
(212) 870-3400

Co-Dependents Anonymous
P.O. Box 33577
Phoenix, AZ 85067-3577
(602) 277-7991

Cocaine Anonymous
3740 Overland Ave. #H
Los Angeles, CA 90034
(800) 347-8998

Gamblers Anonymous
P.O. Box 17173
Los Angeles, CA 90017
(213) 386-8789

Narcotics Anonymous
World Service Office
P.O. Box 9999
Van Nuys, CA 91409
(818) 780-3951

Nicotine Anonymous
World Services
P.O. Box 591777
San Francisco, CA 94159-1777
(415) 750-0328

Overeaters Anonymous
World Service Office
P.O. Box 748
San Pedro, CA 90733
(310) 547-1570

Sexaholics Anonymous
P.O. Box 111910
Nashville, TN 37222
(615) 331-6230

CHRISTIAN SUPPORT GROUPS

Internet Web Site: Christian Recovery Connection
http://www.tfs.net/~iugm

Internet Directory of Christian Support Groups
http://www.tfs.net/personal/iugm/nacr/christian.htm

Living Free
P.O. Box 1026
Julian, CA 92036
(619) 765-2355

National Association for Christian Recovery
3960 Prospect Ave., Suite T
P.O. Box 922
Yorba Linda, CA 92686-0922
(714) 528-6227

Overcomers Outreach, Inc.
520 N. Brookhurst, Suite 121
Anaheim, CA 92801
(714) 491-3000

CHOOSING AN ADD COACH

by Susan Sussman, M.Ed., & Nancy Ratey, Ed.M.

Before contacting an ADD coach, a potential client should have a clear picture of what he or she wants and needs from the coaching relationship. Clients' needs vary tremendously. Similarly, coaches often choose to specialize in specific areas. For example, coaches may specialize in areas such as time management, organizing in the home and/or office, clutter control or budgeting. Therefore, finding a good client/coach match is in large part a result of how well the client is able to articulate his or her needs.

The client should interview a potential coach carefully prior to agreeing to an initial meeting. These questions should be asked by a client when interviewing a potential coach:

- What percentage of your practice is devoted to individuals with ADD?
- How long have you been doing ADD coaching?
- I have identified the following as one of my coaching needs. . . . What is your experience in this area?
- How do you prefer to work (only in face-to-face meetings, by telephone or through electronic mail)?
- How often do you anticipate that we might need to meet/speak?
- What are your fees?
- How and when is payment due?
- Can you provide me with the names of references? (These may be either previous clients who have given the coach permission to use their names as a reference and/or professional colleagues who are familiar with the coach's work.)
- When would you be available for an initial interview?

Coaches should be prepared to spend some time answering clients' questions and describing their unique professional interests and strengths. The client should come away from the informational interview with both answers to their factual questions and a sense of the coach as a person—what a professional relationship with that particular coach would be like. Both clients and coaches will benefit from the give-and-take of a good informational interview since both have the same goal—finding a good client/coach match.

CHOOSING AN ADD COACH is excerpted from: "Coaching Matters," Vol. 1, No.2.
Published by: THE NATIONAL COACHING NETWORK, Box 353, Lafayette Hill, PA 19444
Founders and Directors: Susan Sussman, M.Ed. CompuServe 75471,3101 and Nancy Ratey, Ed.M. CompuServe 74472,62
For more information on becoming an ADD coach or subscribing to "Coaching Matters," please download COACH.TXT from Library 21, PR, Press Releases. Phone and fax number: 610-825-4505. Presently, NCN makes only collect return phone calls.

HOW AN ADD COACH CAN HELP

by Stephen M. Smith, M.Div.

Julie has been on the recovery journey for eight years. Her family intervened and took her to a treatment center. There she learned that she had self-destructive behavior that interfered with her relationships with God, herself, and others. She took that first step and admitted she had a problem she couldn't fix. She asked for help and got it. She learned where the problem first showed up in her life, examined her childhood relationships with her family, discovered the abuse, went to therapy, attended twelve-step meetings, and has been a member of the National Association for Christian Recovery for years. She called one day to say, "What do I do now?, I feel stuck!"

Greg has been a member of twelve-step groups for a while too, and has served in many capacities, such as arranging for recovery speakers to come to his church. Greg has worked the Steps backwards and forwards, is grateful for the progress he has made, but still wants more. "Is going to meetings for the rest of my life all there is? I'll admit it's better than some alternatives, but I want more out of life!"

These questions sound very familiar to me because I have asked them myself. Two years ago I became a professional personal coach, and since then I have heard such questions over and over. "Julie" and "Greg" are composite personalities of many people I have coached. "If I hear one more time that I just need to go to more meetings, I'm going to scream!" said Carla when I first interviewed her over the phone. "I want my life to be more than this. I am deeply grateful for what I've learned, but what do I do now? How do I take all that I've learned and create a new life based on *my* values, and not on what I 'should' be doing?"

Her question is one that more and more people are asking. Twelve-step recovery has helped them see that they don't have to settle for life the way it has always been. Most of these people still go to twelve-step meetings and plan to continue, but they say they are ready to put their newfound tools into action and rebuild their dreams. The problem is that they can find few resources to help them. This is why professional coaches are beginning to play an important role in the recovery world. Coaches are helping people design, build, and enjoy the lives they have recovered.

Thomas Leonard, a former financial planner, founded Coach University in 1992 to train coaches. Since then the coaching profession and its associations have grown dramatically—not through advertising, but by word of mouth. *Newsweek* and the *NBC Nightly News* have carried recent stories about the profession. There are coaching specialties in business management, the arts, recovery, ADD, sales, and many other categories.

Addiction is an equal opportunity disease, affecting people from all walks of life. Recovery groups have been very successful in drawing people from different backgrounds into fellowship to address a common problem. Coaches, because they too have followed the path to recovery, have much in common with the people they counsel.

Coaches can serve as healthy role models. They brainstorm with their clients and help them solve problems. They encourage their clients and push them to make their dreams come true. Coaching is intensely proactive. It is geared for people who are ready to make a shift in their lives and are willing to go for it.

Coaching is not the same as sponsorship in the recovery sense. Coaching is a fee-based service that encourages clients (ADD or otherwise) to see themselves as integrated individuals filled with potential. Coaches help clients put their potential to work by setting quantifiable, achievable goals. Although most coaches who have ADD clients have the disorder themselves, they bring much more to the table than their own struggles and experience. ADD coaches are trained to help clients organize their space, their time, and their inner world. Adept at problem solving, they provide expertise as well as support for their clients.

Stephen M. Smith, M.Div., is a professional personal coach with the International Coaching Federation. For more information about his services call (800) 944-4769 or refer to his home page on the Internet: Stephen @growcoach.com.

APPENDIX THREE

COMMON SYMPTOMS

- We are easily distracted and have difficulty paying attention. We have a tendency to tune out or drift away.
- We are impulsive, and make hasty decisions without considering the consequences.
- We are restless, often hyperactive, and full of nervous energy.
- We have a strong sense of underachievement, and always feel that we fail to live up to our potential.
- We have difficulty in relationships.
- We are procrastinators, and have trouble getting started or feeling motivated.
- We cannot tolerate boredom, and are always looking for something to do.
- We have difficulty getting organized.
- We are impatient, and have a low tolerance for frustration.
- We have mood swings with periods of anxiety, depression, or loneliness.
- We worry excessively, and often have a sense of impending doom.
- We have trouble going through established channels or following proper procedure.
- We have many projects going simultaneously, and have trouble following through with a project or task.
- We are poor observers of ourselves, and are often unaware of our effect on others.
- We tend to say what comes to mind without considering the timing or appropriateness of the remark.
- We have a tendency toward addictive behavior, and use mood-altering substances to medicate ourselves.
- We have difficulty in the workplace. We either change jobs frequently or have trouble getting along with our co-workers.
- We have a family history of ADD or other disorders of impulse control or mood.

COMMON TRAITS

- We have feelings of low self-esteem that cause us to judge ourselves without mercy.
- We are fearful, anxious, and insecure in many areas of our lives.
- We do not give proper attention to our physical well-being.
- We have sudden outbursts of anger, often with loss of control.
- We are resentful, and blame others for our problems and struggles.
- We are either irresponsible or we are overly responsible.
- We are perfectionists, and put undue pressure on ourselves to perform.
- We can be indifferent, and demonstrate an "I don't care" attitude.
- We use rebellion and defiance as a way to disguise the ADD traits that make us feel "different" from others.
- We are defensive and respond poorly to personal criticism or teasing.
- We have difficulty in sexual relationships; we use sex as a source of high stimulation, or we consider sex uninteresting or a bothersome distraction.
- We have a compelling need for excitement and high stimulation in our lives.
- We use co-dependent and caretaking behavior to feel better about ourselves and avoid abandonment or rejection.
- We use denial as a survival tool to protect ourselves from reality.
- We use manipulation and control to manage our lives and make our ADD symptoms more tolerable.
- We tend to isolate ourselves and feel uncomfortable around other people.
- We have a strong desire to escape from the ADD characteristics that negatively affect us.

POSITIVE QUALITIES

- We are intelligent, and highly motivated by intellectual challenges.
- We are creative and highly imaginative, and can express ourselves in unique ways.
- We have high energy and meet challenges with enthusiasm.
- We are intuitive and can easily sense the needs and feelings of others.
- We are resourceful, and can devise ways and means to accomplish things.
- We are warmhearted and enjoy doing things for others.
- We are humorous and have an ability to make others laugh.
- We are hardworking, and have a never-say-die approach to life.
- We are willing to take risks, and see risk-taking as a form of excitement.
- We are loyal, honest, and trustworthy.
- We are flexible, and adapt easily to change.
- We are change agents, and like the intrigue involved in change.
- We are good observers of the world around us, and are able to find quick solutions to complicated situations.
- We are productive and effective if we like what we are doing.
- We are forgiving, and rarely hold grudges.

GUIDELINES
FOR GROUP PARTICIPANTS

Recognize that your Higher Power is in charge.
■ Gratefully acknowledge the presence of your Higher Power and pray for guidance and direction.

Make a point of offering love in an appropriate manner.
■ Respect the needs of others by asking permission to express concern with a hug or a touch. Many people are uncomfortable with physical contact.

Focus individual sharing on the step, exercise, or topic being covered.
■ Focus sharing on individual experience, strength, and hope as it relates to the material being discussed.
■ Allow equal time for everyone in the group to share.

Limit talking and allow others to share.
■ Keep your comments brief; take turns talking; and don't interrupt others.
■ Respect each person's right to self-expression without comment.

Encourage comfort and support by sharing from your own experience.
■ Do not attempt to give advice or rescue the person who is sharing.
■ Accept what others say without comment, realizing it is true for them. Assume responsibility only for your own feelings, thoughts, and actions.

Refrain from cross-talk.
■ Cross-talk occurs when two or more people engage in dialogue that excludes others. It discourages others from participating.

Maintain confidentiality.
■ Keep whatever is shared in the group confidential to ensure an atmosphere of safety and openness.

Avoid gossip.
■ Share your own needs and refrain from talking about a person who is absent.

Refrain from criticizing or defending others.
■ Lovingly hold others accountable for their behavior only if they ask you to do so.
■ Recognize that you are accountable to your Higher Power, and it is not your place to defend or criticize others.

Come to each meeting prepared and with a supportive attitude.
■ Before each meeting, read the designated materials and complete any written exercises.
■ Ask your Higher Power for guidance and a willingness to share openly and honestly each time you communicate with at least one other group participant.

MILESTONES IN RECOVERY

- We are using resentments, fears, and worries as a means to self-understanding, and not blaming others for our shortcomings.
- We are enjoying peace and serenity, trusting that God is guiding our recovery.
- We are gaining a healthy sense of self-esteem and accepting responsibility for our own thoughts, feelings, and actions.
- We are feeling comfortable with our impulsive nature and learning to use it in positive ways.
- We are structuring our lives to combat scattered thinking and disorganization.
- We are accepting distractibility as part of who we are and allowing ourselves extra time in our day for distractions.
- We are no longer fearful of others and have stopped isolating ourselves as a way to protect ourselves and escape from others.
- We are learning to laugh about our forgetfulness and are finding clues to help us remember where we put things and where we are going.
- We are becoming more patient and recognizing that God's timing is always right.
- We are no longer bucking the system; we are learning that we can accomplish more through cooperation than we can through resistance.
- We are taking on fewer responsibilities and trying to reduce the number of projects we have going simultaneously.
- We are using our sense of humor to feel more comfortable in social settings.

THE PROMISES

- We are going to know a new freedom and a new happiness.
- We will not regret the past nor wish to shut the door on it.
- We will comprehend the word *serenity*.
- And we will know peace.
- No matter how far down the scale we have gone, we will see how our experience can benefit others.
- That feeling of uselessness and self-pity will disappear.
- We will lose interest in selfish things and gain interest in our fellows.
- Self-seeking will slip away.
- Our whole attitude and outlook upon life will change.
- Fear of people and of economic insecurity will leave us.
- We will intuitively know how to handle situations that used to baffle us.
- We will suddenly realize that God is doing for us what we could not do for ourselves.

ADD PRAYER FOR PEACE

God, grant me the grace to surrender,
So I can have peace for today.
Take away my fears and worries.
Give me faith that all is okay.

You know my need to fret, to fear.
You know I always expect the worst.
I need more faith, more confidence,
To know your power is at work.

Today you have a plan for me,
And I know your plan is best.
So if I drift or wander or stray,
Draw me back to your loving nest.

Keep me focused on your presence.
Keep me full of joy and light.
Your plan for me is always best.
And your ways are always right.

Today, I'll watch your plan unfold,
I will remember that you're working.
I'll reject the urge to brood and fret,
And find true peace in trusting.

PRAYER OF
SAINT FRANCIS OF ASSISI

Lord, make me an instrument of your peace!
Where there is hatred—let me sow love
Where there is injury—pardon
Where there is doubt—faith
Where there is despair—hope
Where there is darkness—light
Where there is sadness—joy
O Divine Master, grant that I may not so much seek
To be consoled—as to console
To be loved—as to love
for
It is in giving—that we receive
It is in pardoning—that we are pardoned
It is in dying—that
We are born to eternal life.
Amen

SERENITY PRAYER

God, grant me the serenity
To accept the things I cannot change,
The courage to change the things I can,
And the wisdom to know the difference.

Reinhold Niebuhr

THE TWELVE STEPS
OF ADD ANONYMOUS

Step One: We admitted we were powerless over ADD— that our lives had become unmanageable.

Step Two: Came to believe that a Power greater than ourselves could restore us to sanity.

Step Three: Made a decision to turn our will and our lives over to the care of God as we understood God.

Step Four: Made a searching and fearless moral inventory of ourselves.

Step Five: Admitted to God, to ourselves, and to another human being the exact nature of our wrongs.

Step Six: Were entirely ready to have God remove all these defects of character.

Step Seven: Humbly asked God to remove our shortcomings.

Step Eight: Made a list of all persons we had harmed, and became willing to make amends to them all.

Step Nine: Made direct amends to such people wherever possible, except when to do so would injure them or others.

Step Ten: Continued to take personal inventory and when we were wrong promptly admitted it.

Step Eleven: Sought through prayer and meditation to improve our conscious contact with God as we understood God, praying only for knowledge of God's will for us and the power to carry that out.

Step Twelve: Having had a spiritual awakening as the result of these Steps, we tried to carry this message to others, and to practice these principles in all our affairs.

THE TWELVE TRADITIONS
OF ADD ANONYMOUS

1. Our common welfare should come first; personal recovery depends upon ADD Anonymous unity.

2. For our group purpose there is but one ultimate authority—a loving God as God may be expressed in our group conscience. Our leaders are but trusted servants; they do not govern.

3. The only requirement for ADD Anonymous membership is a desire to manage life with ADD.

4. Each group should be autonomous except in matters affecting other groups or ADD Anonymous as a whole.

5. Each group has but one primary purpose—to carry its message to the adult with ADD who still suffers.

6. An ADD Anonymous group ought never endorse, finance, or lend the ADD Anonymous name to any related facility or outside enterprise, lest problems of money, property, and prestige divert us from our primary purpose.

7. Every ADD Anonymous group ought to be fully self-supporting, declining outside contributions.

8. ADD Anonymous should remain forever nonprofessional, but our service centers may employ special workers.

9. ADD Anonymous, as such, ought never be organized, but we may create service boards or committees directly responsible to those they serve.

10. ADD Anonymous has no opinion on outside issues; hence the ADD Anonymous name ought never be drawn into public controversy.

11. Our public relations policy is based on attraction rather than promotion; we need always maintain personal anonymity at the level of press, radio, and films.

12. Anonymity is the spiritual foundation of all our traditions, ever reminding us to place principles before personalities.

Regular Meeting Format

Welcome: "Welcome to *The Twelve Steps—A Guide for Adults with ADD* Step Study. My name is ——————. I am an adult with ADD, and I am your leader for tonight."

Prayer: "Please join me for a moment of silence, after which we will recite the (Serenity Prayer or ADD Prayer for Peace)."

Readings: "I have asked —————— to read the (Common Symptoms or Common Traits)."

"I have asked —————— to read The Twelve Steps."

"I have asked —————— to read The Twelve Traditions." (First meeting of month)

"I have asked ——— to read the Guidelines for Group Participation."

Contributions: "Our tradition is to be self-supporting through our own contributions. We ask for your contribution at this time."

Introductions and preparation: "Let's take time to go around the room and introduce ourselves by first name only. If you are here for the first time, explain briefly why you are here and what you hope to achieve by participating in this Step Study."

"Tonight we will be discussing Step ——— starting on page ———. At this time we will break up into small groups of ——— people each. To determine your group, count off by number, then join the group that matches your number."

Small group sharing: "When you are seated, select a person to be the timekeeper and establish a time limit for sharing, based on the number of people in your group. You will have 45 minutes to read and discuss the material. Cross-talk is discouraged. Cross-talk occurs when two people have a dialogue that excludes other group members. Sharing is most valuable when you focus on your own personal experience, using 'I' statements. I'll give a three-minute warning before it is time to rejoin the large group. Remember to introduce yourself by your first name before sharing."

Large group sharing: "The meeting is now open for general sharing. If anyone has a positive experience to share, please do so at this time. It is always helpful to hear stories of progress and success. When sharing, include ways in which the Steps helped you to function more effectively. Please raise your hand before sharing."

Conclusion: "I have asked _____ to read (Milestones in Recovery, the Promises, or Positive Qualities)."

"Are there any announcements?"

"Next week we will be discussing Step ____. May I have a volunteer to lead next week's meeting?"

"Maintain contact during the week with your sponsor, recovery partner, or someone who is supportive of what you are doing. An alternative to meeting in person is talking on the telephone. You are encouraged to attend other twelve-step meetings as part of your journey."

"An important part of the recovery process is working with a sponsor or recovery partner. If anyone here tonight needs help in finding a sponsor or recovery partner, please see me after the meeting. If there is anyone here who would like to volunteer to be a sponsor or recovery partner, please also see me at the end of the meeting."

"If we sincerely want to change our lifestyle, we use the Steps daily and continue to interact with others in recovery. Interaction with others reminds us that we are not unique—that everyone gets upset occasionally and no one is always 'right.' Through this awareness, we develop the ability to forgive, understand, and love others for who they are and where they are in their lives. We will grow to see how pointless it is to become angry, allow others to inflict emotional pain on us, and harbor resentments. If we stay committed to working the Steps and staying in contact with others, we will gain a sense of dignity and respect for ourselves and others."

Closing: "Reminder! Who you see here, what you hear here, stays here. It is not for public disclosure or gossip."

"Please join me in the closing prayer." (Serenity Prayer, ADD Prayer for Peace, The Lord's Prayer, or Prayer of Saint Francis of Assisi)

Note: The suggested time allocation for the meeting is two hours, divided as follows:

Welcome, prayer, and readings:	10 minutes
Contributions, introductions, and preparation:	10 minutes
Small group sharing:	45 minutes
Large group sharing:	40 minutes
Conclusion:	10 minutes
Closing:	5 minutes

When you are ready for the next leg of your recovery journey, try The Twelve Steps–A Key to Living with ADD. It is a workbook that provides questions and exercises for helping you manage your ADD-related behavior. It includes worksheets for measuring your progress, and is great for teamwork.

Books are available at your local bookstore, or can be ordered direct by calling 1-800-873-8384.

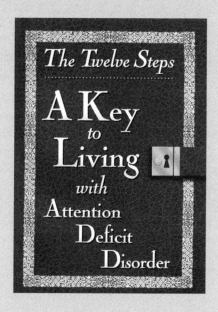